Rice and Spice

To my wonderful funny and clever mum
who encouraged me to cook as a child,
and didn't mind me messing up her
kitchen or baking equipment

Rice and Spice

A Bengali food adventure

ANNA KOCHAN

Caddington Press

First published in 2017 by Caddington Press

ISBN 978-0-9957681-0-9

A CIP catalogue record for this book is
available from the British Library.

Design: Anna Kochan & Blacker Design
Printed in Slovenia on behalf of Latitude Press

We would welcome any comments or feedback,
please email us at **cookbook@futurehope.net**

Contents

Acknowledgements

I am indebted to the Future Hope cooks for their patience in explaining the recipes, particularly Krishna but also Lokhi, Prabha, Pushpah and Sumitra.

I am also grateful to Anil, Bandana, Basudev, Champa, Flower, Libby, Ranjana, Sanjay and Sanjib for sharing recipes with me.

My thanks to Chetna for the warm welcome she gave me to the Future Hope cooking club, and to Dolly, Erica and Sujata for their culinary wisdom.

I owe so much, to so many friends and family who came and tasted my food and reacted so enthusiastically to it, and to Kim and Harold for their tireless and careful checking of my texts.

A huge huge thankyou is due to Sophie Grandage for sharing her stunning Kolkata photographs with me, and to Mike and Roy for their patient advice on food photography.

And most of all, I would like to thank the funny, sparky, mischievous and totally adorable children at Future Hope for making my stay in Kolkata so memorable.

I am also very very grateful to Mike at Blacker Design who, together with Emma, turned my words and photographs into such a beautiful book.

Foreword

So much of my life is taken up in travelling the world in pursuit of cricket and reporting back to the British public what is happening to their team. Through 'Test Match Special' I meet incredible people and see amazing places and every so often come across an extraordinary organisation which makes a huge impact on the lives of others.

It was in December 2012 when I was in Kolkata, India, reporting on the Test Match being played at Eden Gardens that I came across Future Hope, a charity that takes the most destitute children from the railway lines and streets and gives them a home and opportunity. I interviewed the Founder, Tim Grandage and Swapan, one of the children and this was broadcast during the lunchbreak next day. If any charity is worth supporting, it is Future Hope. You only have to meet the children to see how their lives are being turned around by good all-round education and a caring, nurturing environment. These children are sparky, fun loving and real survivors; they are also passionate about cricket! They have a will and determination to succeed, and most of them turn out to be responsible adults with good jobs who give back to society. If only all the underprivileged children in India could experience a Future Hope upbringing.

Anna Kochan, a British cricket fan who heard the report on Test Match Special, was moved by it and decided to go to Future Hope in India as a volunteer. She stayed for six months working with the children and saw how crucial good food was to their development. She has written RICE AND SPICE using the secret recipes that she gleaned from the Future Hope cooks, and is donating all proceeds to Future Hope. It is a real labour of love!

Jonathan Agnew MBE
BBC Cricket Correspondent

A Bengali food adventure

My Bengali food adventure started early one bleak December morning. Switching on the radio I am transported to Kolkata where the BBC's cricket correspondent Jonathan Agnew is filling the lunch break in the England v India test match with a report on his visit to Future Hope. I am spellbound. This charity founded by former British banker, Tim 'uncle', sweeps the streets of Kolkata for vulnerable children, giving a home and education to the most needy in the city. It is a fascinating story. And much to my joy, the charity welcomes volunteers.

The formalities completed, the date is fixed for my departure. And, on 1 October, 2013, I am on my way. For 6 months, I breath the air of Kolkata, I tread the streets of Kolkata and I eat the food of Kolkata. In this book, I share with the reader the recipes for the Bengali food that is cooked and eaten every day at Future Hope's school and children's homes. Additional recipes come from pupils, teachers and friends I meet along the way.

The day I arrive in Kolkata, my Bengali food adventure starts in earnest. By lunchtime, I have already had a tour of the school, met the teachers and am queuing up with an excited crowd of children to go into the dining room. I follow the others and take a *thali* (metal tray) and pass slowly along the line of teachers dishing out the food.

There's no menu, there's no choice. My *thali* fills up with rice, *dal*, egg curry and cabbage *chechki*. I then join the children sitting on benches at long trestle tables. And we eat with our fingers. Everyone eats with their fingers, not just the children, but the teachers, the principal, the guests, just everyone. I watch how the children do it and try to emulate their deft little fingers and how they squeeze the rice and curry into neat little bundles that they then lift to their mouths. And then at the end, when no solids remain, they put the *thali* to their lips and tip the remaining tasty juices down their throats. It seems a waste to leave it. The Future Hope school *dal* is much-loved but it is very liquid. So, how do the rest of us deal with it? Well, I did see one of the principals slurping up his remnants, like the children – but not in their sight. It takes me many months to eat rice and curry in this way, and I am frequently reprimanded by the children for using my left hand, which is strictly taboo.

At the end of the meal, we rinse our *thalis* and wash our hands in communal sinks outside the hall.

My adventure takes on new challenges in the evening when I am a guest at one of the Future Hope children's homes. We don't just eat with our fingers, but have to do so sitting cross-legged on the floor with the *thali* sitting on the floor in front of us. It's an impossibility for me. But my hosts, some ten chatty and vivacious little girls aged 5 to 11 and their houseparent make me feel most welcome. And the dinner, composed of more rice, more curry and more spicy vegetables is utterly delicious. The children have a rota for housework, and once we have eaten, two girls wash up our *thalis* and then scrub the floor.

A tiny kitchen nestled in one corner of Future Hope's main school hall provides the lunches for pupils and staff during the week, and dinners for the two children's homes that are on the same site. That means roughly 270 lunches and 50 dinners every day. Cooking smells from the kitchen emanate throughout the school from late morning onwards. They are almost always mouthwatering. But not invariably. Sometimes the mustard oil used for frying gives off the most lung-shattering fumes. It's a phenomenon you are likely to come across frequently in the streets of Kolkata, where mustard oil is the norm and where cooking on the street is common.

The Future Hope food is without exception good, tasty and greatly appreciated. I hear not one child complaining during the 6 months I am there. And I enjoy it immensely. However, I am sure disasters must occur from time to time and after much prodding, a couple of children mention an incident when the oil caught fire, the fish was ruined and they had to eat eggs. It was Tim 'uncle' who came to the rescue, the children say. He happened to be passing when the fire started and he grabbed the fire extinguisher and put it out.

Providing the varied and tasty meals at Future Hope is the task of a small team of cooks. They are local women who have learnt to cook from their mothers and grandmothers, and their style of cooking is nothing but authentic Bengali. This means lots of potato, and a sprinkling of turmeric and sugar in everything.

The cooks' first job every morning is to go to the market to buy the fresh vegetables needed for the day's meals. The cooks do not know what they are going to cook any day until they see what's on offer at the market. But there are certain patterns. The Friday lunch menu always includes an egg dish and Friday dinner a chicken dish. All lunches and most dinners feature rice and *dal*, but dinners on Wednesday have *roti* (*chapati*) and *luchi* (*puri*), on alternate weeks. Of course, seasonality plays a certain part. I am in Kolkata during the cooler months so unripe papaya, which is widely available, is used in many of the mixed vegetable dishes. Sadly, I miss the mango season which is at the height of summer. Everyone tells me of the wonderful chutneys that the cooks make with the mangoes from the trees that grow in the school grounds.

Kolkata is in the coastal state of West Bengal and water is plentiful despite almost no rainfall from the start of November to the end of April. So, the cooks returning from the market have inevitably found an abundance of large succulent cabbages, cauliflowers, carrots, onions, potatoes, green beans, pumpkin, spinach and tomatoes, often aubergine, green peas and beetroot, sometimes okra too. Not everything every day, of course.

Once they've changed into their work saris, and donned aprons, the cooks begin the work of vegetable preparation. Indian cooking is quick and easy once all the vegetables are cleaned, peeled and cut, and the spices all weighed out. The cooks are lovely, warm and motherly women, who sit and chat companionably as they work. Their language is Bengali but Krishna, who's English is better than the others, translates for me when there is big news to report, such as the birth of a grandchild.

The tool most commonly used for vegetable preparation is a *boti*, which resembles a small sickle mounted on a wooden block. The user, in a squatting position, holds the block down with the foot, so has both hands free to hold the vegetable and cut it against the blade. It is good for cutting anything from a tiny clove of garlic to a large chunk of pumpkin.

Shape is everything in Bengali cooking. My friend Flower, who I meet through the Kolkata Jewish community, tells me that when she was a child, she could tell what they would be having for dinner from the shapes of the vegetables the cook was preparing.

In between watching the cooking procedures and noting down recipes for the cookbook, I try and help. Mostly I shell peas and eggs. That's many kilos of peas and several hundred eggs. I have tried helping

with other jobs but using a *boti* takes skill. After a short scary attempt to master it, I ask for a knife. But though potato peelers are easily found in the kitchen, knives are not. In fact, this kitchen seems to possess only one knife, a very long not-so-sharp knife, and it is kept under lock and key in a high cupboard that requires the cook to climb on a chair to access. I rarely see it being used and then it is for cutting paneer (a very soft cheese) into precisely sized blocks.

A highlight of my Bengali food adventure is the Future Hope staff picnic. It starts with an early morning bumpy ride in the school bus to Rajarhat, the designated site for Future Hope's new campus. At the time, it is little more than a few fields with crops and cows, a fishpond, and a temporary toilet block. But, in preparation for our picnic, various awnings have been erected. Inside one are the trestle tables and benches where we are served our breakfast and lunch. Inside the other is a temporary kitchen where local villagers cook our food.

The first meal of the day is a breakfast made up of freshly fried *luchi* accompanied by spicy potato, washed down with hot sweet *chai* (tea). There is hardly time for a game of cricket before the bar opens, and more snacks appear. This time it's cauliflower *pakora* (cauliflower florets dipped in batter and deep-fried). Not long after, trays of deep-fried whole fish, taken straight from the pond are handed round, followed shortly after by plates of raw vegetables, tomato, cucumber, onion. But this is not yet lunch, which comes a little while later – more fish, chicken, pulau rice, *dal*, aubergine and lentil bake. It is an abundance of the most outstanding Bengali food. Today, the Rajarhat site supplies Future Hope's kitchen with fresh vegetables during the winter months.

The British have left a huge mark on Kolkata's eating habits, at least among the small most well-to-do element of the population. The menus offered in the city's many private clubs provide such treats as prawn cocktail, meat loaf, cauliflower in white sauce, vegetables au gratin, Russian salad, garlic bread, bread pudding, caramel custard..... They also serve much sought-after pork and beef dishes such as leg of ham and steak. As the religious Muslim population eats no pig meat and the Hindus no beef, most of the meat eaten in Kolkata is mutton or chicken. The bars at Kolkata's clubs are also much valued. Here you can drink even on a Thursday when Kolkata's liquor stores are closed.

On my first visit to a club, I sit with my host Mr S, sipping tea from china cups and eating cucumber sandwiches. The bread is rather thick but the crusts have been cut off, and I enjoy them hugely. It's a welcome change from rice and spice. Here, inside a high boundary wall, we are protected from the noise and bustle of a busy city, and it feels immensely civilised. As the sun sets behind the well-manicured cricket pitch in front of us, the overweight of Kolkata arrive for their evening walks. Mr S tells me that clubs such as these are a 'British contribution to India. They are just like your country clubs.' Later Mr S orders 'fish fry' which turns out to be a plate of fish fingers, served with tomato ketchup.

The clubs are at the centre of affluent Kolkata social life, offering a wide range of events. I go to a political debate, a literary evening and even a cookery demonstration. On this occasion, the proprietor of a well-known Bengali restaurant in Kolkata cooks a sample of her most popular recipes in front of us. Her food is extremely good. But, my companion, another renowned Bengali cook, is tutting throughout. Well, the restauranteur frequently tastes her cooking apparently using the same spoon with which she is stirring the food.

Where I am living in Kolkata as a PG (paying guest), the kitchen facilities are limited. Just two gas rings. When I feel the need for western style food, I make a thick vegetable soup or a salad. I've been told to be cautious regarding the tap water, so I wash all fresh fruit and vegetables with potassium permanganate to take care of any impurities. At times I am overcome by an urge to cook something sweet, and experiment with recipes for fudge and crystallised citrus peel. But there is a limit to what you can do in a saucepan. If I could only find an oven, I would be able to initiate baking activities with the children, which is so much fun for everyone and massively educational.

In fact, Indian homes rarely possess an oven. Indian food is cooked on a stove in a wok-type pan. However, hidden away in one of the Future Hope children's homes is an old-fashioned standalone cooker with oven below and gas hob on top. We connect it up to a gas cylinder and find that it works. And so the young girls and I make cupcakes, chocolate and banana cakes, and shortbread and a variety of cookies. The children are more accustomed to mixing food with their hands but they quickly adapt to using a spoon. On a healthier note, we cook apple crumble but it is not an unqualified success. The children do not like the apple as they are not used to it being cooked, although they are happy to eat the crumble.

On hearing of our exploits, the boys' houseparent is keen to have me bake with his charges too. And so he arranges for the cooker to be transferred to the boys' home. That means taking it down four flights of stairs and transporting it a couple of miles through the streets, nothing that a few strong lads can't manage.

Eating out in Kolkata can be an adventure, particularly if you opt for street food. The choice is massive and the quality excellent, although I must confess that I only frequent street stalls to which I have been recommended by a native of Kolkata. My friend Mrs D cautions me not to eat *jalebi* unless I am with her as she knows which stalls use orange dye fit for consumption and which use textile-grade dye. Happily, I suffer no ill-effects at any time during my stay.

Western influences are starting to appear in the cuisine of Kolkata, mainly in the form of cafes and cake shops. International burger and pizza chains are also venturing into the market. Pizzas are not the greatest because there is simply no appropriate cheese available. India's dairy products are truly superb, the milk, the butter, the yoghurt – or curd, as they call it, and paneer, the soft cheese. You have to go to a particular stall in New Market to find a hard cheese. It's a smoked one that comes in small patties, and it is smooth and creamy and divine. But, if you want a cheese that will bubble and melt and go brown on the top of a pizza, the only option is a very expensive imported product.

One momentous event to take place during my Bengali adventure is the opening of Quest, a shopping mall close to my lodgings. It is huge and smart, and many international brands are due to arrive here, such as Burberry and Bodyshop. But I am only interested in Spencer's, a huge supermarket in the basement. Here there is imported cheese, sausages and bacon, as well as a motley selection of other foreign goods including Rose's marmalade, Bird's custard powder, Tetley tea bags, Ambrosia tinned rice pudding and custard, Bisto instant gravy and Tate & Lyle golden syrup.

At Spencer's, many things are fascinating such as the boxes of double-yolk eggs and the numerous varieties of oats; so many different types of dried fruit, even strawberries and kiwi fruit, but no glace cherries; and a fantastic display of citrus fruit but no lemons as we know them. It's also curious to see a huge tank where you choose a fish for your aquarium located right next to the counter where you buy your fish for dinner. The fish is all beautifully cleaned, priced and labelled, and displayed on a heap of crushed ice.

Buying fish at the local market is, of course, much more exciting, if a little nerve-wracking. A kindly English-speaking vendor at a chicken stall leads me deep into the heart of the market to an area full of fish stalls that I would never have found myself.

The chicken man and the fish man discuss between them what I should buy, and thus I come home in great excitement with a whole fish, head and all. One of my landlady's servants is happy to take the head. I cook the fish and it is most tasty and succulent.

Markets both small and large abound in Kolkata. They are busy and colourful, and joyous places to wander. And, if you need help carrying your shopping bags, you can usually find a porter – or coolie, as my Bengali friend calls them. The porter accompanies you round the market, loading your purchases onto a huge round flat basket that he transports on his head.

As Christmas approaches, fruit cakes start to appear in the shops. Although only a small percentage of the population is Christian, Christmas is a bank holiday and the festival is widely celebrated. Even Annapurna, my tiny chaotic corner store, stocks a range of fruit cakes. But, I'm told, the best is to be found in Kolkata's huge New Market at Nahoum's, a bakery founded some 115 years ago by Baghdad Jews. The cakes, which are essentially rich fruit cakes without marzipan or icing, are certainly very popular. On Christmas Eve, queues snake up and down the aisles outside the shop until stocks run out. Mrs B, an administrator at Future Hope, brings us in a sample of her own Christmas cake. Like most in Kolkata, she does not own an oven and has taken her cake to a local bakery to be cooked.

Christmas is a lovely time to be in Kolkata. The skies are blue and the sun is warm rather than hot. It is curious to see children in Santa Claus hats eating popcorn, candyfloss or ice cream, and having sleigh rides on a perfect green lawn. The occasion is a party for underprivileged children that one of the clubs has organised.

Future Hope takes a break at Christmas but just before the holiday the children celebrate with a Mela. It's one long party at which the children entertain each other and local residents with music, dance, drama, comedy and acrobatics. Children's art and craftwork is on sale, so too are many different types of food, all made by the children. You can discover many of their recipes in the pages that follow, as well as recipes for the food that is cooked every day at school. Bon Appetit!

Tips and Techniques

I have written the recipes in RICE AND SPICE exactly as they were told to me in Kolkata. The only variation is in the quantity of **chilli**. Indian food tends to be hot and spicy, which is not to everyone's taste. So most of my recipes give a choice. If you are worried about your food being too 'hot', make sure to use the smallest quantity of chilli, particularly where red chilli powder is concerned. You can also remove the seeds from the inside of both dried red chillies and fresh green ones to reduce their effect. Or you can leave the chilli out altogether because all the recipes have lots of other flavoursome ingredients and the food will still be tasty, if not so authentic. I personally use minimum amounts and chillies without seeds.

It is always possible to make last minute adjustments such as adding extra chilli powder 10 minutes before the end of the cooking time, if the food is too bland, and adding a little sugar or lime juice, if the dish is too 'hot'. Another tip is to keep a stock of fresh green chillies in the freezer. They freeze very well as long as you remove the stalk and stub first and take them straight from the freezer when you need them for cooking.

The recipes in RICE AND SPICE are mostly quite simple to make, and do not rely on much previous cooking experience. One feature of Indian cooking that is rarely encountered in European cuisine is the use of **paste**. Many of the recipes call for paste made from different combinations of onion, garlic and ginger, and sometimes green chilli too. The paste is easy to make by whizzing up the specified quantities of the ingredients in a liquidiser or food processor with a small amount of water. Alternatively, use a pestle and mortar to reduce them to a mush. This works well for small quantities of garlic and ginger but it is best to chop them finely first. The other option is to buy jars of minced garlic or ginger, or tubes of puree, which are available in major UK supermarkets.

Deep frying is also a feature of Indian cooking, particularly in the snacks recipes. Many of us probably do not do this at home very often, but it is not complicated, and the results are hugely worth the effort. It is crucial to get the oil to the right temperature before starting frying otherwise the food will not turn out crisp and brown. The method I use for checking the temperature is to drop a tiny

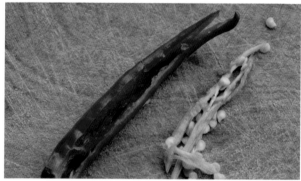

blob of food into the oil. If the food immediately starts to sizzle and bob around on the surface of the oil, the temperature is right. If it drops to the bottom with hardly a trace, then it is not hot enough.

In Kolkata, the main type of **oil** in use is mustard oil, which is available in the UK although the label on the bottles indicates it is not suitable for culinary purposes. I cook with vegetable or sunflower oil instead. A useful hint is to re-use leftover oil and store it for future use. Once it has cooled, simply pour the leftover oil through a sieve but try and keep back as much of the dregs that has collected at the bottom of the pan as possible. The oil that has come through the sieve should be almost clear. Keep it in a sealed jar.

All the recipes in RICE AND SPICE have been tried and tested in my kitchen in London using local ingredients. The vast majority of the ingredients are easily available in the major supermarkets though some of them may be unfamiliar. In the introductions to individual recipes, I have indicated a few, such as the **masalas** (packaged spice mixes) that might be difficult to source. Again, if you leave them out, the food will still taste delicious but will lose some of its authenticity. If you do manage to

buy them, use with caution. They can be extremely 'hot' depending on the brand. The glossary that follows this introduction provides explanations of some of the less familiar ingredients.

The recipes are not complicated but, for the best results, it is vital to follow the specified order for adding the ingredients. It can make a significant difference to the taste, especially where spices are concerned. For example, if turmeric is added to very hot oil, it is likely to give food a bitter taste.

The lists of ingredients are sometimes frighteningly long because of the variety of spices. However, once the spices are measured out and the vegetables prepared, the cooking time is usually very short. To save time and energy, you can use tinned chickpeas, tinned or frozen spinach puree, frozen peas, and jars of ready prepared garlic and ginger paste, all of which are widely available.

When time is short, **rice** is easier to cook than one of the Indian breads and goes well with everything, particularly those dishes that have a lot of gravy. For the best fluffy rice, it's a good idea to soak the grains in plenty of water before cooking. Opinions vary about soaking time but 30 minutes should be sufficient. Cooking time is then shortened.

The **breads** are more of an effort to make but very well worth it. It is important to use warm water when mixing the dough.

If you are preparing a meal for eight people, or more, then you might serve both bread and rice, and a great variety of dishes. The quantities of servings given with each recipe are a rough guide only. Indian meals are usually served as one course that is made up of a whole range of dishes including rice or bread; dal; fish, chicken or egg; one or two vegetable dishes; a salad and a chutney.

If you want to offer guests a starter, most the recipes in the Soup and Snacks section would be suitable. Similarly the recipes in the Tea and Sweets section could act as a dessert. As for drinks, it is not usual to have **alcohol** to accompany a meal. According to my friend Flower, mixing alcohol with chilli makes both more powerful. So, people tend to drink before eating.

Many of the recipes in RICE AND SPICE are ideal for cooking with children. The sweet recipes on pages 146, 152, and 154 and salads on pages 59, 62 and 65 are particularly good because they are simple, and no cooking is involved. Children also love to make the bread recipes and fried snack recipes although adult supervision of the cooking would be necessary.

Finally, a wok is an ideal cooking pot for most of the recipes in RICE AND SPICE.

Glossary of unfamiliar ingredients

AMCHUR: a fine beige coloured powder made from unripe green mangoes. It has a sour and fruity taste.

ASAFOETIDA (also known as hing): a fine primrose yellow coloured powder made from the gum of a vegetable tap root. It gives food a subtle leek flavouring.

ATTA FLOUR: wholemeal flour made from wheat, which has been finely milled. It is used in Indian bread recipes.

CAROM SEED (also known as ajwain or bishopsweed): looks like a smaller form of cumin seed and tastes strongly of thyme.

CHAPATI FLOUR: the same as ATTA, see above.

FENUGREEK: a herb and a spice. The leaves are used in Indian cooking either fresh or dry. The seeds are one of the five ingredients in the distinctive Bengali panchphoran spice mix.

Asafoetida

Carom seed

GHEE: a form of clarified butter that is used in Indian cooking. You can buy tins of ghee in major UK supermarkets but it is well worth making your own because it tastes so much better.

GRAM FLOUR (also known as besan flour or chickpea flour): widely used in Indian cooking, particularly in fried food. It is made from chickpeas and is therefore gluten free. I advise sieving gram flour in recipes where you need to mix it with water to form a smooth batter, because it has a tendency to cake.

JAGGERY (also known as gur): brown sugar made from the sap of a palm tree or from sugar cane, usually sold as a solid brown lump.

NIGELLA SEED (also known as kalonji seed or black onion seed): looks like onion seed, tastes a bit like onion, but is no relation to the onion family.

PANCHPHORAN: a five spice mixture that is specific to Bengali cooking, and widely sold in the UK. The five are black mustard seed, cumin seed, fennel seed, fenugreek seed and nigella seed. Often used in vegetable dishes, the combination of spices gives food a distinctive flavour.

PANEER: a mild, soft cheese used in cooking. Paneer is often cut into cubes and fried before being added to a curry. It is sold in UK supermarkets in small vacuum-packed blocks. Sometimes it is referred to as cottage cheese or curd cheese.

SOYA CHUNKS: made from soya beans, they are used as a vegetarian alternative to meat. Soya chunks are sold in a dried form and have to be rehydrated in boiling water before cooking.

TAMARIND: the fruit of the tamarind tree that is used in Indian cooking to give food, particularly chutneys, a tart taste. You can buy slabs of the dried tamarind pods and rehydrate them but it is much easier to use jars of tamarind concentrate, also readily available.

Fenugreek

Nigella seed

Panchphoran

Fried paneer

Soya chunks

Chapati – Roti

Enough for 15–20 roti

500g atta flour or chapati flour
1 teaspoon salt
Warm water, to mix

Chapati, also known as roti, is the Indian flat bread that often accompanies a meal instead of rice. It is a soft and floppy bread that you tear bits off to scoop up dollops of curry. If you are lucky enough to be a guest at a Future Hope home on a Wednesday evening, you will probably be offered roti with your dinner. In the Future Hope kitchen, roti are finished over a bare flame which gives them an extra roasted-flour flavour.

Mix the flour and salt in a large bowl. Gradually add enough warm water to form a dough. If you pour in a ladleful of water at a time, and stir it into the flour with a knife, you will know that the quantity of water is about right when the flour starts forming clumps. Now, use your hands and knead it into a soft elastic dough. If it feels too stiff, add more water. If too sticky, add more flour.

Now take pieces of dough the size of a large egg and form into small patties. Then, using a rolling pin and plenty of flour to stop the dough sticking, roll each patty into a thin round (1–2mm thick, 15–20cm across).

To cook the roti, first warm a flat-bottomed frying pan. Place one of the roti in it and let it cook for about half a minute. Turn it over and, as the second side starts to cook, the roti will puff up. You need to pat it down to push the air out. Finally, turn the roti over and finish cooking the first side. A cooked roti will be speckled with golden brown patches.

To keep the roti warm while you finish cooking, wrap them in foil or a clean tea towel.

Leftover roti can be warmed up and eaten on another day. First sprinkle them with a few drops of water then briefly heat in a hot frying pan, turning once.

Fenugreek Paratha – Methi Paratha

Enough for 20 parathas

250g atta flour or chapati flour
100g gram flour
50g fresh fenugreek (or fresh coriander), washed and finely chopped
1 teaspoon red chilli powder
Carom seed, a pinch
1 teaspoon sugar
2 teaspoons salt
2 tablespoons oil, plus extra for frying

A paratha is a flat bread that is a rich form of roti because it contains oil, and is also partly cooked with oil. The parathas in this recipe are packed full of fresh herbs and are particularly delicious. You can use fresh fenugreek leaves but if this is unavailable, the recipe works equally well with fresh coriander.

First mix the atta and the gram flour. Then add the fenugreek leaves (or coriander). Use your finger tips to pinch the leaves into the flour to release the flavour. Stir in the chilli powder, carom seeds, sugar and salt. Add the oil and enough warm water to make a dough that is soft and pliable but not too stiff. To do this, follow the same technique as for the roti on page 33.

Take pieces of dough the size of an egg, and roll into a ball.

Now, lightly dust a clean surface with flour and, using a rolling pin, roll each ball of dough into a round of about 15cm diameter.

To cook the fenugreek parathas, follow the same technique as for the stuffed parathas on page 39.

Poori – Luchi

Freshly cooked luchi are hot and crispy yet soft and succulent. I love cooking them. Although it does contain oil, the dough is very similar to that of a roti, and is just as easy to make. The main difference is that luchi are deep-fried and, when the pale slivers of dough hit the hot oil, they turn as if by magic into great puffs of gold.

Also known as poori, luchi are eaten as an alternative to rice at a meal – but usually only on special occasions because they are rather rich. In the best Indian restaurants, trays of freshly-fried luchi are handed round continuously.

Enough for 20 luchi

250g plain flour
250g atta flour or chapati flour
1 teaspoon salt
2 teaspoons sugar
Bicarbonate of soda, a pinch
50ml oil plus extra for
   rolling and frying

Mix the flours together and add the salt, sugar and bicarbonate of soda. Now add 50ml of oil and sufficient warm water to obtain a soft pliable dough. To do this, follow the same technique as for the roti on page 33.

Form the dough into balls the size of walnuts. Then, with a lightly floured surface and a rolling pin, roll the balls of dough into thin rounds about 8–10cm in diameter. Have a bowl of oil at hand and dab drops of oil onto the patties as you roll them out.

To fry the luchi, you will need a deep pan or wok containing oil to a depth of 5cm. Heat the pan on a medium heat and when the oil starts to sizzle,

gently put in the luchi, a couple at a time. They will start to puff up. You will need to quickly turn them over and rapidly remove them from the oil when they become crisp and golden brown all over. Continue cooking the luchi, keeping the oil on a medium heat and adding the slivers of dough quickly, one after the other.

It is useful to keep a dish filled with sheets of absorbent kitchen paper by your side to put the cooked luchi onto when they come out of the oil. The paper will absorb any excess oil.

Serve immediately.

Enough for 18 parathas

FOR THE DOUGH
500g atta flour or chapati flour
2 teaspoons salt
2 tablespoons oil

FOR THE FILLING
500g potatoes, boiled,
   peeled and mashed well
125g onions, chopped very finely
½–1 green chilli, sliced
   very finely
1 teaspoon amchur
½–1 teaspoon red chilli powder
1 teaspoon salt

Stuffed Paratha – Aloo Paratha

For a special treat, make these stuffed parathas. The mildly spicy filling containing mashed potato and onion is soft and crunchy. They are surprisingly easy to make and guests are sure to be highly impressed.

To make the filling, simply mix all of the filling ingredients together.

Now make the dough by mixing the salt and flour, then adding the oil and enough warm water to make a dough that is soft and pliable but not too stiff. Follow the same dough-making technique as for the roti on page 33.

Take pieces of the dough, the size of an egg, and roll into a ball. You should have about 18.

Now, lightly dust a clean surface with flour and, using a rolling pin, roll each ball of dough into a round of about 15cm diameter. Put a large tablespoon of the filling mixture into the centre of each round and draw up the edges of the dough to form a small parcel with the filling inside. Make sure to pinch the edges of the dough together. Turn the parcel over so that the joins are on the underside and gently roll it back out into a round of

15cm diameter. It does not matter if there are small tears in the dough and the filling is visible.

To cook the parathas, you will need a flat-bottomed frying pan. Warm the pan on a medium heat, then add a paratha. Cook it for about a minute then turn it over. While the second side starts to cook, brush the first side with oil. Now turn the paratha over again and brush the second side with oil. Once the first side is golden brown, turn the paratha over again and cook until the second side is also golden brown.

As each paratha finishes cooking, wrap it in foil or a clean tea towel, to keep warm. But they are best served immediately.

Coriander and Chilli Chutney

Liquidise a large bunch of fresh coriander with 2 or 3 green chillies and 2 or 3 cloves of garlic. Add salt to taste, and it is ready to use. One of the more healthy of chutneys, the heat of the chilli and garlic perfectly complements the fresh herby taste of the coriander. It is a tasty addition to sandwiches, and is an excellent accompaniment to curries and rice dishes. It should be stored in an airtight container, and will keep in the fridge for four or five days. As an alternative, use a mixture of mint and coriander.

Sweet and Sour Chutney

Dissolve 200g jaggery over a gentle heat in a saucepan with 200ml water and 50g amchur, stirring from time to time. Once the jaggery has dissolved, bring the mixture to the boil and simmer gently for 5–10 minutes, still stirring. It will thicken slightly. Now roast a teaspoon of cumin seed in a dry frying pan. Grind the seed to a fine powder and add to the chutney. Cook for a few extra minutes. You can also add a pinch of red chilli powder, or more, if you like. This chutney has similar uses to the date and tamarind recipe above. Bengali jaggery made from palm sap is not easily found in the UK: jaggery made from sugar cane works almost as well and is more readily available. It is often sold as a solid coffee-coloured lump. Amchur is a light brown powder made from dried unripe mango, which has a tart fruity taste. It is sold in many UK supermarkets.

Date and Tamarind Chutney

Liquidise 2 cups of dried dates with a little warm water until completely smooth, ensuring that all stones have been removed first. Mix in enough tamarind paste until the sweetness of the dates is just balanced by the tanginess of the tamarind. The amount of tamarind paste will depend on the strength of the tamarind paste and the variety of the dates used. I make this chutney with medjool dates and the result is perfection. Cumin powder, ground ginger and red chilli powder are often added to this chutney but I prefer it without. It has a thick, sticky consistency, and goes particularly well with any of the snacks that have yoghurt among their ingredients. Keep the date and tamarind chutney in a screw-top jar in the fridge and it will last for a few weeks.

Tomato Chutney

Heat one tablespoon of oil in a large pan until very hot. Fry a pinch of panchphoran and one dried red chilli in the hot oil until brown. Now add 1kg of roughly chopped tomatoes and two teaspoons of salt. Bring to the boil then cover and simmer for 10 minutes, stirring occasionally. Finally mix in 200g sugar and cook gently for another 10 minutes, still stirring. This is not a thick chutney but it is a stunning red colour, and the sweet tomato flavour is deliciously offset by a subtle spiciness. I have eaten it as part of a Future Hope lunch. It was served hot, ladled onto my *thali*, alongside a dollop of rice and a couple of vegetable curries. It was really tasty just mixed with the rice.

Tomato and Coriander Chutney

This chutney is utterly delicious. It has a taste that is all its own, neither tomato nor coriander. In my opinion, it is not just the ideal accompaniment to any Indian meal, but is wonderful eaten with cheese or cold meat, like the kinds of chutney we are more accustomed to in the UK. I have experimented with bottling it like a preserve, and storing it for more than a year, and it works well.

50g oil
500g onion, very finely
  chopped
500g sugar
1kg tomatoes, cut into 1/8ths
2 teaspoons salt
2 bunches fresh coriander,
  leaves only, finely chopped
4 green chillies, cut in half
  lengthwise

First heat the oil in a very large pan. Once it starts to spit, add the onion and turn the heat down. Cook until the onion becomes transparent but do not allow it to burn. Add the tomatoes and stir well. Add the salt, and then the sugar, and stir well again. Now mix in the coriander leaf. Bring to the boil while stirring. Turn down the heat and gently simmer the chutney, stirring from time to time. It should take about 20 minutes to cook. The chutney is ready when it has turned a deep brown colour and the onion has softened. Throw in the green chillies and cook a further 5 minutes.

This chutney can be bottled and kept for more than a year. Simply transfer the still-warm chutney to warm sterilised jars and seal with a lid. As the jars cool, you should hear a satisfying little pop, indicating that a vacuum has formed. Once opened, use within a couple of weeks as the chutney will grow mould quite quickly!

Bread Rissoles with a Spicy Potato Filling – Aloo Tikki

Makes 20–25 rissoles

2 teaspoons cumin seed

2 teaspoons coriander seed

5 very large potatoes, boiled and peeled

2 onions, finely chopped

50g fresh coriander, washed and finely chopped

2 teaspoons salt

Juice of 1 lime

Red chilli flakes, a large pinch

30 square slices of plain white, or brown bread, crusts removed

Oil for frying

In this recipe, a typically Bengali spicy potato filling is enveloped in a crisp and crunchy layer of bread. In India, they call this deep-fried snack a bread roll. As well as a snack, they can be eaten hot as a starter, served with chutney or with a tomato or chilli sauce. You should start with slightly more slices of bread than you need because sometimes the assembly process goes wrong! It works best with slices of bread that are square and have had their crusts removed.

First roast the cumin and coriander seeds in a dry frying pan until they start to brown. Grind the seeds to a fine powder.

Now mash the potato in a large bowl. Mix in the chopped onion and fresh coriander. Then, using your fingers, pinch the mixture to release the flavours of the onion and coriander. Mix in the salt, the lime juice, the chilli flakes and the ground spice mixture. Taste and adjust seasoning if necessary.

To assemble the rissoles, you will need a bowl of water at hand. Take a slice of bread, and dip all four edges quickly into the water. Then place the slice of bread flat between your palms and gently squeeze out any excess water. Now put the slice of bread down on the table and place a ball of the potato filling at its centre. The quantity of filling should be just enough so that when you fold the corners of the bread up over it, the edges meet and overlap just very slightly. Once you have folded the corners around the filling, take the rissole in your hands and roll it around gently so that the bread closes up completely around the filling and it forms a perfect sphere. Repeat until all the filling has been used.

To fry the rissoles, you will need a large frying pan or wok containing oil to a depth of 5–6cm. Heat the pan and once the oil starts to sizzle, fry the balls in batches of four or five. They will turn a deep brown colour. Remove from the oil, drain well and transfer to a bed of absorbent kitchen paper. Serve hot with chutney, or tomato or chilli sauce.

Crackers Topped with Potato, Yoghurt and Chutney – Papri Chaat

Crisp crackers, tender potato, creamy yoghurt and sweet-sour chutney, the combination is totally mouthwatering. The crackers alone are addictive. They are flavoured with carom seed, giving them a distinctive taste of thyme. Add the topping and you have a deluxe snack. Papri chaat also make a great starter.

Enough for 20–25

200g plain flour
1 teaspoon carom seed
1 teaspoon salt
2 tablespoons oil plus extra for frying
10 small potatoes, boiled, peeled and diced
3 onions, finely chopped
30g fresh coriander, washed and finely chopped
1 litre plain yoghurt
200g date and tamarind chutney
   (or sweet and sour)
Cumin powder for sprinkling
Red chilli powder for sprinkling

First make the crackers (papri). Mix the flour with the carom seeds and salt, and add the oil and enough water to form a firm dough. You will need about 100ml of water. Now take pieces of dough the size of a walnut and roll them into round disks about 6cm across. Prick them well all over, using a fork, and they are ready to fry. You will need a large frying pan or wok containing oil to a depth of 3–4cm. Make sure the oil is very hot, then fry the papri, in batches of three or four, until golden brown on both sides. Drain the papri well as you remove them from the oil. Now transfer to a bed of absorbent kitchen paper.

When the papri have cooled down, arrange them on a serving plate. Mix the diced potato with the finely chopped onion and coriander, and divide the mixture among the papri. Put a blob of yoghurt on each one then drizzle the chutney over the top, and sprinkle with a few grains of cumin powder and red chilli powder. Serve immediately.

Lentil Pakora – Moong Dal Pakora

These tasty lentil patties have a subtle flavour that is due in part to the use of asafoetida, a spice I encountered for the first time at the Future Hope cooking club. Readily available in the UK, it is a pale yellow powder tasting a bit like leek. These patties are good as a snack or starter, served hot with coriander and chilli chutney.

250g split yellow lentils
   (moong dal)
5g asafoetida
½ teaspoon salt
50g fresh coriander, washed
   and finely chopped
2 or 3 green chillies, finely
   chopped
Oil, for frying

First soak the dal in water for 2–3 hours. Now wash it thoroughly and drain well, then liquidise it with enough water to create a thick paste. Combine the asafoetida, salt, fresh coriander and green chilli with the paste, and form it into small round patties about 2cm across.

To cook the patties, you will need a large frying pan or wok containing oil to a depth of 4–5cm. Heat the pan until the oil is sizzling, then drop dessertspoons of the mixture into the oil and fry the patties in batches of five or six until golden brown. Remove the patties from the oil, drain well and transfer to a bed of absorbent kitchen paper.

Serve hot with coriander and chilli chutney (see page 41).

Lentil Soup – Libby's Dal Soup

10–12 servings

2 tablespoons olive oil
2 onions, finely chopped
1 large carrot, peeled
   and diced
Garlic/ginger paste, made
   using 12g garlic and
   30g ginger
Small piece cinnamon stick
2 cardamom pods, bruised
   to release flavour
2 teaspoons panchphoran
1 dried red chilli
5 tomatoes, roughly chopped
500g chickpea dal (chana dal),
   soaked overnight
For garnish: mustard
   seed, curry leaves, fresh
   coriander, yoghurt

In India, dal is a sauce rather than a soup. Sometimes very watery, sometimes very thick, it is made with one or another kind of pulse, and is served as an accompaniment to rice and other dishes. A liquid and tasty dal sauce is served every day at Future Hope lunches. This recipe for a dal soup has been adapted by Libby who, along with her husband Mike, worked at Future Hope in the early 2010s. You can make the soup as thick or as thin as you like, by adding more or less water. And try it with different pulses, dried peas and/or lentils. Each one has its own particular flavour and texture.

Heat the oil in a large pan. Add the onion and carrot, and cook 10 minutes, stirring occasionally. Add the ginger/garlic paste, then cinnamon, cardamom, panchphoran and red chilli, and lastly the chopped tomato. Stir well and cook a few minutes. Wash the chickpea dal well and add it to the pan, together with enough water to cover. Bring to the boil than simmer until vegetables and dal are cooked. Cool slightly.

Remove the cinnamon stick and cardamom pods then liquidise the dal. If you prefer, leave it fairly lumpy. Add more water if you want the soup more liquid. Taste and adjust seasoning. Bring to the boil. Sprinkle with finely chopped fresh coriander, and serve garnished with a generous dollop of yoghurt, and a scattering of fried curry leaves and mustard seed.

Onion Fritters – Onion Pakora

Enough for 20–24 pakoras

1kg onion, finely sliced
500g gram flour
1 teaspoon red chilli powder
1 tablespoon sugar
2 teaspoons salt
Oil, for frying

Crisp and crunchy on the outside, moist and tender in the middle, onion pakoras are a typical Indian snack. I serve them with tomato and coriander chutney (see page 42), and my guests love them. So do the children at Future Hope where onion pakoras are a lunch dish.

First prepare the onions. I find it easiest to cut the onions in half lengthways and to slice them holding them cut-side down on a board. You then have half rings.

Now mix together the flour, chilli powder, sugar and salt in a very large bowl.

Combine the sliced onion with the dry ingredients, making sure individual onion rings are well coated. Now, start adding cold water, a little at a time, until the mixture forms a sticky paste that is just wet enough to hold the onion together.

To cook the pakoras, you will need a deep frying pan or wok filled with oil to a depth of about 5cm.

Heat the oil. When it starts to sizzle, gently drop tablespoons of the mixture into the oil. You should be able to fry three or four at a time. They will bob about on the surface of the oil and you will need to turn them over so that they cook on both sides. They will be crisp and a dark golden brown when they are ready. Drain the oil from the pakoras as you remove them from the pan, and transfer them to a bed of absorbent kitchen paper. Serve with chutney.

As with most fried food, pakoras are most delicious the moment they are cooked. But if you have guests, it may be more practical to make the pakoras earlier in the day and then to heat them up for 10 minutes or so, in a very hot oven, just prior to serving.

Potato Cakes with Green Chilli, Black Pepper and Coriander – Aloo Tikia

Enough for 20 cakes

- 1kg potatoes
- 2 tablespoons cornflour
- 2 teaspoons salt
- 3 teaspoons ground black pepper
- 2–4 green chillies, finely chopped
- 15g fresh coriander, washed and finely chopped
- Oil, for frying
- Chutney and fresh coriander, for serving

These tasty little potato patties are soft and succulent inside and lightly crispy on the outside. Delicately flavoured with green chilli, black pepper and fresh coriander, they make an excellent starter for any meal, served with chutney, and are a good way to use up leftover mashed potato, too.

First peel the potatoes and cook them in salted boiling water until tender. Drain well. Now you need to mash the potato until all the lumps have disappeared. Let it cool down slightly. Meanwhile mix the cornflour with the salt and pepper. Combine the mashed potato with the cornflour, the green chilli and the coriander. Taste the mixture and add more salt if necessary. Form the mixture into small patties. You will need a large frying pan or wok containing oil to a depth of 5–6cm. Start heating the pan and, once the oil is sizzling, fry the patties in batches of four or five. They are ready when they have turned a delicious golden brown. Drain well and transfer to a bed of absorbent kitchen paper. Serve hot with chutney and fresh coriander.

Sandwiches

Sliced white and brown bread of excellent quality can be bought throughout Kolkata, even in small kiosks on the street. Here are a few recipes for Indian-style sandwiches. You could also try eating leftover curries on toast for breakfast, lunch or tea! The Indians do. And they also eat English-style cucumber sandwiches but you will have to take afternoon tea at the Calcutta Cricket & Football Club to find those.

CHEESE, GARLIC AND GREEN PEPPER TOASTED SANDWICHES

Mash 25g butter with 25g garlic, ¼–1 teaspoon red chilli powder and a pinch of salt. De-seed a green pepper and cut into 1cm squares and boil for a few minutes in water, then drain and cool. Cut 125g paneer into 1cm squares. Spread slices of bread with the spiced butter and lay pieces of paneer and green pepper on top. Make into sandwiches, toast and serve.

CUCUMBER AND CORIANDER SANDWICHES

Liquidise a bunch of fresh coriander, a couple of green chillies and a green pepper, with a little salt, to make a paste. Spread on slices of bread with thin slices of peeled cucumber, and make into sandwiches. Toast, if you like.

EGG AND MUSTARD SANDWICHES

Boil 3 eggs for 20 minutes. Remove shells and leave to cool. Mash the eggs with 25g butter and 1 teaspoon mustard powder. Spread on slices of bread and make into sandwiches.

POTATO SANDWICHES

Cook 500g potatoes, then drain and mash. Mix 125g finely chopped onion with the potato, as well as 25g finely chopped fresh coriander, 1 or 2 finely chopped green chillies and ½–1 teaspoon red chilli powder. Make the sandwiches by first spreading the bread with butter, then filling with the spiced potato. Toast, if you like, and serve with chutney.

Spiced Chickpea Salad with Tomato, Cucumber and Potato – Chana Chaat

Enough for 8 servings

250g chickpeas, soaked for
   at least 6 hours
2 small cucumbers, peeled
   and diced
2 tomatoes, diced
1 onion, finely chopped
1 large potato, boiled
   and diced
1–4 teaspoons chaat masala,
   according to taste
Juice of 1 lime
1 teaspoon salt
Red chilli flakes, a small
   pinch (optional)

It is the healthiest recipe in the book and one of the favourites of Future Hope's cooking club. These crunchy chickpeas are combined with crisp chunks of cucumber and tomato and tender diced potato, all delicately seasoned with onion morsels, spices and lime juice. It is exactly the kind of refreshing snack for a hot summer's day. Packets of chaat masala are readily available in the UK but one word of warning – chaat masala can be very spicy, depending on the brand, so it is best to add a little at a time.

Boil the chickpeas until tender. Drain and wash them well, and leave to cool. Now add the cucumber, tomato, onion and potato to the chickpeas, and sprinkle with the chaat masala. Mix well. Sprinkle with the lime juice and salt, and mix again. Add optional chilli flakes just before serving.

Spiced Mashed Vegetable in a Bun – Paw Bhaji

Enough for 8–10 servings

½ cauliflower, split into
   small florets
100g carrots, peeled and diced
100g peas, fresh or frozen
250g potato, boiled, peeled
   and mashed well
2 onions, finely chopped
1 green pepper, de-seeded and
   cut into small pieces
100g tomatoes, roughly chopped
2 tablespoons oil
25g paw bhaji masala
1 teaspoon garlic paste
100g spring onion, finely
   chopped
Juice of 1 lime
50g fresh coriander, washed
   and chopped

A substantial nutritious snack that you might also like to try for breakfast, this is a toasted burger bun filled with a very tasty vegetable mash. If you cannot find the paw bhaji masala that is used to flavour the mash, it is equally delicious with a couple of diced green chilli and a pinch of red chilli powder. If you are able to buy the specific masala, then use it with caution. Add a little at a time, tasting as you go.

First prepare all the vegetables. Bring a large pan of salted water to the boil and cook the cauliflower, carrot and green peas until tender. Drain the vegetables and mix with the mashed potato. While the vegetables are cooking, gently fry the onion, green pepper and tomatoes in the oil. Once the onion and pepper are soft, add the paw bhaji

masala and garlic paste, and cook a few minutes. Mix in the spring onion, and finally add the vegetable mash. Stir in the lime juice and a little water, and cook for another 5 minutes. Taste and adjust the seasoning, then serve the mash hot in a freshly-toasted burger bun with butter and fresh coriander.

Spiced Potato Salad with Tomato, Green Pepper and Onion – Aloo Chaat

Enough for 4 servings

16 small new potatoes,
   boiled and peeled
1 small onion, chopped small
1 large tomato, cut into small cubes
1 green pepper, de-seeded and cut
   in 1cm squares
1 tablespoon lime juice
½ teaspoon sugar
½–1½ teaspoons chaat masala,
   according to taste
1 tablespoon chopped fresh
   coriander

Not dissimilar to the spicy chickpea salad on the previous page, this refreshing salad has potato rather than chickpeas as its main ingredient. Again, take care with the chaat masala.

Combine the potato, onion, tomato and green pepper. Add the lime juice, sugar and chaat masala, and mix well. Sprinkle with the coriander. Chill before eating. Can be served with chutney such as date and tamarind or sweet and sour (see page 41).

Spiced Yellow Pea Salad with Yoghurt and Chutney – Mattar Ki Chaat

200g dried yellow peas,
   soaked overnight
1 teaspoon turmeric
1 teaspoon salt
100g yoghurt
2 onions, finely chopped
1 tablespoon fresh coriander,
   washed and finely chopped
Cumin seed, a small pinch,
   roasted and ground
Red chilli powder, a small
   pinch
25g chutney, date and
   tamarind or sweet and sour

This is street food at its best with a diversity of flavours and textures, not to mention colours that are unique to the pavement stalls that line India's thoroughfares. The creamy yoghurt contrasts deliciously with the sweet tanginess of the rich brown chutney, the piquant spices and sharp crunchiness of the onion, all held together on a solid base of peas.

Boil the peas until tender. Wash and drain well. Mix in the turmeric and salt, and leave to cool. Now put the cooked peas on a serving dish. Spoon the yoghurt on top, and sprinkle with the chopped onion and coriander, ground cumin and chilli powder. Finally drizzle the chutney over the top.

Stir-fry Noodles with Vegetables – Champa's Chow Mein

Enough for 4–6 servings

200g fine egg noodles
4 tablespoons oil
2 carrots, cut into fine
    matchsticks
100g green beans, cut into
    0.5cm lengths
1 onion, finely chopped
2–4 green chillies, finely
    chopped, according to taste
1 green pepper, cut into fine
    matchsticks
200g cabbage, shredded
½ cucumber, cut into fine
    matchsticks
1 onion, finely sliced
Tomato and/or chilli sauce
Fresh coriander, finely
    chopped

Chow mein has been widely adopted by street food vendors in Kolkata although it is mainly associated with Chinese cuisine. I am indebted to Future Hope houseparent Champa for this recipe, which she learnt from her mother. Champa's family often had chow mein for breakfast when she was young, and today Champa makes chow mein for the Future Hope children in her care, sometimes for breakfast at the weekend, sometimes as a Sunday afternoon snack. You can choose which vegetables to mix with the noodles. The following is for guidance only.

Cook the noodles following the instructions on the packet. Drain and set aside on an oiled dish. Heat the oil in a large frying pan or wok. First add the carrot and beans, and fry gently for about 10 minutes. Next add the onion, green chilli, green pepper and cabbage and continue cooking for another 10 minutes. Check all the vegetables are cooked then set aside and cover to keep warm.

Add a little more oil to the frying pan, and heat the cooked noodles gently in it for about 5 minutes until they are hot. Stir in the cooked vegetables, adjust the seasoning, and heat for a further 10 minutes, stirring well.

Lastly mix in the cucumber and onion, and drizzle with tomato sauce or chilli sauce. Sprinkle with the coriander and serve immediately.

Stuffed Omelette Paratha – Basudev's Egg Roll

Enough for 6 servings

200g plain flour
Baking powder, a pinch
10ml oil
10g sugar
Salt, a pinch
Oil for frying
6 eggs
1 onion, finely chopped
½ cucumber, finely chopped
2 large tomatoes, finely chopped
50g cabbage, finely shredded
1 carrot, finely chopped
2 small potatoes, boiled
   and diced
Tomato and/or chilli sauce

The omelette in this recipe is fried onto a paratha then rolled up around a mass of fresh crisp vegetables and drizzled with tomato/chilli sauce. Locally known as an egg roll, it is a delicious and nutritious meal in itself. Many thanks to Future Hope houseparent Basudev, who shared his recipe with me. Together with a team of his boys, Basudev makes hundreds of these egg rolls for Future Hope's end-of-year Mela celebration. Try experimenting with different fillings, for example shredded cooked chicken. And, if you visit Future Hope in Ballygunge, a visit to Dhaba takeaway is obligatory. Their egg rolls are almost as good as Basudev's!

Make the paratha dough by mixing together the flour, baking powder, oil, sugar and salt then adding enough warm water to make a soft pliable dough. Divide the dough into six equal balls. Roll each ball into a disk measuring about 200mm across, then fry them, one at a time, in a flat-bottomed frying pan with a little oil. Cook them for a few minutes on each side till golden brown. Transfer the finished parathas to a plate covered with a cloth to keep warm.

Now, break one egg into a bowl and add a pinch of salt. Beat with a fork to combine egg yolk and white. Heat a little oil in the frying pan then gently pour the beaten egg into the pan. Use a spatula to form the egg into a round shape about the same size as the parathas. Once the egg is partially cooked, place one of the parathas on top of it and continue cooking till the egg is fully cooked. The egg and paratha will have fused together. Turn it over so that the paratha is now on the bottom of the pan, and heat for a couple more minutes.

Finally turn the egg roll onto a plate with the egg side up. Cover with a layer of mixed vegetables. Drizzle with tomato and/or chilli sauce. Roll the paratha up into a cone shape, and it is ready to eat. Repeat with the remaining eggs and parathas.

Tomato and Coriander Soup with Garlic

Enough for 10 servings

1kg fresh tomatoes, cut into
    quarters
100g butter
100g garlic, made into paste
100g fresh coriander, washed
    and finely chopped
1 litre vegetable stock
100g tomato ketchup
1 teaspoon sugar
1 teaspoon salt

Soup is only eaten on special occasions in India. One such special occasion is Future Hope's New Year's Eve party. It is a party of great music, lively dancing and fabulous food. This delicious tomato and coriander soup, served steaming hot, is a most welcome midnight refreshment. The recipe comes from Anil, one of the first young boys to be supported by Future Hope. Now married with two children, Anil runs Momo Junction, a momo cafe in Kolkata's New Market. He often caters for Future Hope celebrations.

Heat the tomatoes in a large pan and boil slowly till they are reduced to a mush. Liquidise the mush and strain through a sieve to remove the seeds and skin. You will now have a puree. Melt the butter in a large pan, and add the garlic paste. Cook gently until the garlic is just starting to brown. Add the tomato puree and the fresh coriander, and cook for a further 10 minutes. Finally add the vegetable stock, ketchup, sugar and salt. Taste and adjust seasoning. Bring to the boil and serve.

Egg Curry

Every morning, Future Hope's cooks go to the market to buy fresh vegetables. They say they do not know what they are going to cook on any one day until they've checked out what's good at the market. On Fridays, however, lunch invariably includes an egg dish and it is often this egg curry. It is simple to make and extremely nutritious. I spent many happy hours in the Future Hope kitchen on a Friday morning shelling eggs for more than 250 hungry kids. Exactly the same sauce can be used to make a soya curry (see below).

Enough for 6 servings

6 eggs
2 tablespoons oil
Ginger/garlic/onion paste, made with 50g ginger, 40g garlic and 2 onions
¼–1 teaspoon red chilli powder
1 teaspoon turmeric
1 teaspoon coriander powder
1 teaspoon cumin powder
80g peas, fresh or frozen
2 small potatoes, peeled and cut into small wedges
½ teaspoon sugar
½ teaspoon salt
2 large tomatoes (or 4 small ones), cut into 1/8ths

Cook the eggs in boiling water for 12–15 minutes. Drain away the hot water and submerge the eggs in cold water. You will now be able to handle them and strip off the shells.

The next step is to make the curry sauce. Heat the oil in a large pan or wok. When it starts to sizzle, add all the paste and spices. Mix well and cook several minutes. Then add the peas and potato, followed by the sugar and salt.

Finally add the tomato to the pan, together with the eggs and enough water to almost cover the eggs. Bring to the boil then reduce the heat and simmer gently for about 10 minutes. Taste and adjust seasoning, then serve with plain rice.

SOYA CURRY

Replace the eggs with soya chunks. For 6 people, you will need about 50g of soya chunks. Pour boiling water over the soya chunks and leave to soak for at least 10 minutes. Then squeeze as much water out of them as possible. Make the curry sauce as for the egg curry above but instead of adding the eggs at the end, add the soya chunks. Simmer gently for about 10 minutes, and serve with plain rice.

Egg with Spiced Spinach

Enough for 6 servings

6 eggs
500g spinach, washed well
2 tablespoons oil
1 onion, finely chopped
Onion/ginger/garlic paste,
**   made with 1 onion, 25g**
**   ginger and 15g garlic**
3 small tomatoes,
**   cut into 1/8ths**
1 bay leaf
½ teaspoon turmeric
½ teaspoon salt
¼ teaspoon sugar
½ teaspoon red chilli powder
½ teaspoon garam masala

Pureed spinach mixed with small chunks of tomato is flavoured with a typical Bengali mix of ginger, garlic and spices. It combines deliciously with hard-boiled egg. Serve with rice for a nutritious and substantial lunch. Exactly the same spiced spinach puree can be used with paneer cheese (see below).

Cook the eggs in a pan of boiling water for 12–15 minutes. Drain off the hot water and cover the eggs in cold water. They should now be cool enough to handle. Remove the shells.

Cook the spinach in 100ml water until it wilts. Remove from the heat and leave to cool. Liquidise to a smooth puree.

Heat the oil in a large pan or wok and fry the chopped onion until it just starts to brown. Add the onion/ginger/garlic paste, and continue cooking for several minutes. Mix in the tomato and bay leaf, and cook a few minutes more. Now stir in the turmeric, salt, sugar and red chilli powder, and cook for a further 10 minutes. Finally, add the spinach puree and cook another 10 minutes. Taste and adjust seasoning. Mix the hard-boiled eggs with the spinach and heat thoroughly. Serve, sprinkled with garam masala powder.

PANEER CHEESE WITH SPINACH

Replace the eggs with paneer cheese. You will need 250g of paneer. Cut it into 1cm chunks, and fry the pieces gently in hot oil for a few minutes to cook them. Once the paneer has browned, remove from the pan, letting as much oil as possible drain off. Add the paneer directly to the hot spinach sauce, and serve.

Omelette Curry

Pieces of omelette and potato float in a lightly spiced curry sauce. Ideal for a lunchtime treat.

Heat 2 tablespoons oil in a deep pan or wok. When hot, add the onion, bay leaf, potato, turmeric, chilli powder, salt, and ginger/garlic paste. Lower the heat, mix well, and cook for 3 or 4 minutes, stirring. Now add 100ml of water. Bring to the boil and add the tomato and sugar. Stir in another 100ml of water. Once boiling, reduce the heat and cook gently until the potato is tender.

Now prepare the omelettes. You can make them as one- or two-egg omelettes. Break one or two eggs into a bowl. Add a pinch of salt and whisk lightly with a fork. Put a drop of oil into a small frying pan and heat gently. Pour the egg into the frying pan, letting it spread out over the base of the pan. Cook until the egg is just dry. Now, fold it over on itself, turn out onto a plate and cut in two or three pieces. Repeat to use all the eggs. Add the omelette pieces to the spicy potato and serve with plain rice or roti.

Enough for 2–4 servings

- 2 tablespoons oil, plus extra for frying omelettes
- 1 onion, sliced
- 1 bay leaf
- 1 large potato, peeled and sliced into 5mm thick half-moon shapes
- ½ teaspoon turmeric
- ¼–½ teaspoon red chilli powder
- ½ teaspoon salt
- 1 tablespoon garlic/ginger paste (made with equal measures of garlic and ginger)
- 1 tomato, chopped
- ½ teaspoon sugar
- 4 eggs

Paneer Cheese in a Piquant Sauce with Garlic and Ginger – Chilli Paneer

Enough for 6–8 servings

2 onions, chopped finely
2 tablespoons oil
Paste made with 50g onion,
    50g ginger and 50g garlic
1 green pepper, de-seeded and
    cut into 1cm pieces
4 tomatoes, cut into 1/8ths
1 tablespoon chilli sauce
1 teaspoon soy sauce
1 tablespoon tomato sauce
1 teaspoon distilled malt
    vinegar
500g paneer, cut into 15mm
    cubes
100g flour
½ teaspoon salt
½ teaspoon baking powder
Oil, for frying
50g salad onion leaves,
    finely chopped

The paneer in this recipe is dipped in batter and fried then submerged in a thick piquant sauce flavoured with garlic and ginger and loaded with tomato and green pepper. It is a Future Hope lunch dish hugely popular with the children. The paneer available in UK stores is a shiny, cream-coloured rubbery slab that is quite unappetising. However, the minute it is cooked, it softens up and becomes irresistible.

First make the sauce. Fry the chopped onion in a large frying pan with two tablespoons of oil until it starts to brown. Add the paste and cook for a few minutes, stirring frequently. Then add the tomato and green pepper, and cook for a few more minutes. Now, mix in the chilli sauce, soy sauce, tomato sauce and vinegar, together with 240ml water. Bring to the boil then reduce the heat and simmer for 20 minutes.

Meanwhile, prepare the paneer. First combine the flour, salt and baking powder. Now gradually add cold water to the flour to make a paste that is sticky but still quite runny. Dip the pieces of paneer in the paste ready for frying. You will need a large frying pan or wok containing oil to a depth of about 3cm. Heat the pan and, as soon as the oil starts to sizzle, start frying small batches of the coated paneer pieces. Once they have turned crisp and golden brown, drain and transfer directly to the chilli sauce. Garnish with the salad onion leaves and serve with plain rice.

Paneer Cheese in a Mixed Vegetable Stew with Tomato and Ginger

Enough for 4–6 servings

2 tablespoons oil

125g green beans, cut into
   1cm pieces

125g carrots, cut in 1cm chunks

125g potato, cut into
   1cm chunks

125g peas, fresh or frozen

½ large cauliflower, cut into
   very small florets, discarding
   the tough stalk

50g tomato paste

½ teaspoon ginger paste

½ teaspoon red chilli powder

½ teaspoon turmeric

½ teaspoon sugar

½ teaspoon salt

1–2 teaspoons subji masala

½ tablespoon black
   mustard seed

125g paneer, cut into
   1cm chunks

Extra oil for frying the paneer

This is a tasty stew to serve with plain rice or roti. A colourful mix of tender vegetables and chunks of paneer (the Indian cheese) are coated in a creamy aromatic gravy flavoured with tomato and ginger. The recipe specifies subji masala, which is not widely available in the UK, but the dish is excellent even without it. If you do manage to buy a packet of subji masala, add it cautiously as packaged spice mixes vary considerably.

Heat the oil in a large deep pan or wok. First add the beans and carrots, and cook for 10 minutes. Now add the potato and peas, and cook for a further 5 minutes. Add the cauliflower, tomato paste, ginger paste, chilli powder, turmeric, sugar, salt and subji masala, and enough water to almost cover the vegetables. Bring to the boil then reduce the heat, cover the pan and cook very gently until all the vegetables are just cooked. Taste and adjust seasoning.

Meanwhile, make a paste with the mustard seeds and a few pieces of the paneer. Heat a few tablespoons of oil in a frying pan and when it starts to sizzle fry the rest of the paneer for a few minutes until it turns golden brown. Add the paste and the pieces of paneer to the vegetables. Mix well and serve.

Scrambled Egg with Tomato, Coriander and Green Chilli – Egg Bhurji

Enough for 2 servings

4 eggs
Pinch of salt
½ onion, finely chopped
1 tablespoon peas, fresh or
**   frozen**
1 stem fresh coriander,
**   washed and finely chopped**
1 tomato, chopped
2 green chillies, finely
**   chopped (into rings)**
2 tablespoons oil

This colourful Indian version of scrambled egg is flavoured with coriander, green chilli and tomato. During the week, lunch is always available at Future Hope homes for houseparents and children who are not in school. The cook might well make them egg bhurji.

Break the eggs into a bowl and whisk well with the salt to combine the yolks and whites. Add all the other ingredients apart from the oil. Now heat the oil in a non-stick frying pan and pour in the egg. Cook on a medium heat and use a wooden spoon to move the egg around in the pan until it is cooked throughout and no liquid egg is left. Serve immediately with toast or roti.

Soya Chunks with Tomato and Green Pepper in a Piquant Sauce – Chilli Soya

Enough for 6 servings

50g soya chunks
2 tablespoons oil
1 onion, finely chopped
Paste made with 50g onion, 20g ginger and 20g garlic
1 teaspoon salt
¼ teaspoon red chilli powder
1 green pepper, cut into 1cm pieces
4 small tomatoes, quartered
2 tablespoons distilled malt vinegar
2 tablespoons soy sauce
40g cornflour
¼ teaspoon ground black pepper
40g salad onion leaves, finely chopped

These soya chunks are coated with a thick piquant sauce that is full of tomato and green pepper. The Future Hope cooks call the dish chilli soya although chilli is only one of the many flavours. There is also ginger and garlic, vinegar and soy sauce, and black pepper. Soya chunks are frequently used in Indian vegetarian cooking, and are not difficult to buy in the UK. I recommend the small rounded chunks that measure about 12mm.

Pour boiling water onto the soya chunks and leave for at least 10 minutes. Drain and squeeze as much of the water out of the soya as you can.

Now make the sauce. Heat the oil in a large deep pan or wok. Add the finely chopped onion and fry until it starts to brown. Mix in the onion/ginger/garlic paste together with the salt and chilli powder. Cook for several minutes, while stirring. Then add the green pepper and tomato, followed by the vinegar and soy sauce. Add 240ml water and bring to the boil then reduce heat and simmer for about 20 minutes. Add the well-squeezed soya pieces to the sauce, and pour in enough water to almost cover them. Cook gently for another 10 minutes.

Finally, using a small bowl, add enough water to the cornflour to make a loose paste. Mix this in with the soya and bring to the boil, stirring continuously while the sauce thickens. Stir in the black pepper and spring onion, and serve with plain rice.

Biryani Chicken – Chicken with Egg, Potato and Rice

Enough for 6–8 servings

1kg chicken (about 9 pieces, on the bone but skinned)
Paste made with 4 onions, 50g ginger and 40g garlic
100g yoghurt
½ teaspoon salt
1–2 teaspoons biryani masala
50ml oil
4 or 5 small new potatoes
8 eggs
500g basmati rice
100g butter
1 teaspoon rosewater

Biryani is a meal in itself. This aromatic dish contains not just chicken and rice but also hard-boiled egg and potato, all flavoured with ginger, garlic and spices, as well as a hint of rosewater. To make life easy, this recipe uses biryani masala, pre-packed spices specially mixed to create a biryani flavour. It is available in many of the major UK supermarkets.

Mix together the chicken, onion/ginger/garlic paste, yoghurt and salt and 1 teaspoon of biryani masala. Leave to marinate for about 30 minutes.

Meanwhile, boil the potatoes, whole and in their skins. When cooked, remove the skins. Cook the eggs in boiling water for 12–15 minutes and remove the shells. Put the rice to soak in water for at least 10 minutes.

Now, heat the oil in a large pan or wok. Add the chicken and marinade, and cook on a gentle heat for 20 minutes, stirring from time to time. Taste, and add more biryani masala or salt if you like.

While the chicken is simmering, cook the rice with salt. It should be slightly undercooked. Strain well.

The next step is to assemble everything. You will need a very large saucepan with a tight-fitting lid. First melt 50g butter in the saucepan then put in a layer of chicken, followed by a layer of rice, then another layer of chicken, and another layer of rice, and finally arrange the eggs and the potato on the top. Sprinkle with the rosewater. Cover the pan tightly, and cook on a very low heat for about 10 minutes. This final steaming process diffuses the flavours around the pot. At Future Hope, the cooks make a thick paste of flour and water that they roll into a long sausage-shape and put around the rim of the pan to create a seal when they place the lid on top.

Chicken Curry

Enough for 8 servings

50ml oil

20 cloves

3 cardamom pods, bruised to
    release flavour

Small piece of cinnamon stick

2 bay leaves

2 large tomatoes, cut into
    quarters

1 tablespoon turmeric

½ tablespoon sugar

½ teaspoon – 1 tablespoon red
    chilli powder

1 tablespoon cumin powder

1 tablespoon coriander
    powder

½ teaspoon salt

1kg chicken pieces (on the
    bone but skinned)

A smooth velvety sauce brimming with cinnamon, clove and
cardamom flavours envelops the chicken in this recipe. It is
exceptionally quick and easy to make. One of my favourites. Try
including the chicken stomach and liver, as they do at Future Hope.

Heat the oil in a large deep pan till very hot. Now add all the
ingredients (apart from the chicken) in the order listed, mixing as you
go. Stir well. If you have chicken stomachs, add them now and cook
on a gentle heat for 10 minutes. Then add the chicken pieces and stir
well to ensure they are coated with the sauce. Do not worry if there
is hardly any sauce at this stage as the chicken releases juices as it
cooks. Cover the pan and continue cooking on a gentle heat for about
45 minutes. Taste and add more salt, if necessary.

Chicken with Green Pepper and Tomato in a Piquant Sauce – Chilli Chicken

Enough for 6–8 servings

1kg chicken, cut into small
    pieces, no skin or bone
1 egg, lightly beaten
25g cornflour
50ml oil
2 onions, chopped finely
Paste made with 50g onion,
    50g ginger, 50g garlic
2 green peppers, de-seeded,
    cut into 15mm squares
1 tablespoon chilli sauce
1 teaspoon soy sauce
1 tablespoon tomato sauce
1 teaspoon distilled malt
    vinegar
4 tomatoes, cut into 1/8ths
½ teaspoon sugar
½ teaspoon salt
Black pepper, a pinch
50g salad onion leaves,
    roughly chopped

MARINADE:
Paste made with 50g ginger,
    50g garlic and 50g onion
1 teaspoon distilled malt
    vinegar
1 teaspoon soy sauce
Black pepper, a pinch

At Future Hope they call it Chilli Chicken. It contains only a little chilli and lots of ginger and garlic, and spices. Full of flavour, the chicken pieces float in a delicious thick sauce, full of green pepper and tomato, and also soy sauce, demonstrating how oriental cuisine has influenced Bengali.

Combine the marinade ingredients together in a large bowl and mix in the chicken pieces until they are thoroughly coated. Leave to marinate for 30 minutes. Now add the egg, 12.5g cornflour and a pinch of black pepper, and mix well. Heat 50ml oil in a wok, or deep frying pan, and fry the marinated chicken pieces individually until they start to turn a light golden brown. Set fried chicken aside on a plate and discard any marinade that is left. Clean the cooking pot thoroughly.

The next step is to make the sauce. Using the clean cooking pot, heat 50ml oil and fry the chopped onion until it starts to brown. Add the garlic, ginger and onion pastes (50g of each), and mix well. Continue cooking until it starts to brown too. Add the green pepper, soy sauce, vinegar, tomato sauce and chilli sauce. Mix well and simmer on a low heat for 10 minutes. Now add the tomato and the chicken and enough water to just cover. Simmer for another 15 minutes. You should now taste the sauce and add salt, if you want, and the sugar. Finally, using a small bowl, mix the remaining 12.5g cornflour with enough cold water to make a smooth loose paste, and add to the chicken. Stir well until it thickens just slightly. Serve with a garnish of black pepper and salad onion leaves.

Coriander Chicken

Enough for 6–8 servings

1kg chicken pieces, on the
    bone but skinned
Juice of 1 lime
50g garlic/ginger paste, made
    with 25g ginger and 25g
    garlic
½ teaspoon salt
2 tablespoons oil
2–3 green chillies, slit
    lengthways
10g turmeric
10g cumin powder
250g fresh coriander,
    liquidised with 50ml water

The coriander and lime in this recipe give the chicken an exciting citrus and herb flavour. I am indebted to former Future Hope student Sanjay for it. Now building a successful career in the hospitality industry, Sanjay started cooking when he was about 8 years old. 'It was the custom in the village for women to be quarantined when they were menstruating. I was the eldest child in the family. So, my mum would have to sit in a corner as far away from the kitchen as possible, and I would do the cooking,' he says. But, Sanjay adds, he cannot take full credit for the coriander chicken recipe as he learnt it from Future Hope cook Prabha, adding a few touches of his own.

Put the chicken pieces into a large bowl. Drizzle with the lime juice, and mix with the garlic/ginger paste and salt. Leave to marinate for about an hour.

Heat the oil in a large deep pan. When hot, add the green chillies and fry a few minutes. Now add the chicken, followed by the turmeric and the cumin powder. Stir well and cook for about 15–20 minutes on a low heat, stirring frequently. If it starts to stick on the bottom of the pan, add a little water, but only a little. As soon as the chicken is cooked all the way through, add the liquidised coriander, and cook on a low heat for a further 5 minutes. Taste and adjust the seasoning.

Slow-cooked Chicken with Onion and Spices – Chicken Kosha

Enough for 8 servings

50ml oil, plus extra for frying
4 onions, finely chopped
Paste made with 40g garlic
and 50g ginger
1 teaspoon cumin powder
1 teaspoon coriander powder
1 teaspoon turmeric
¼–1 teaspoon red
chilli powder
½ teaspoon salt
2 bay leaves
1kg chicken, cut into
medium-sized pieces
(on the bone but skinned)
Garam masala to garnish

Chicken kosha is a typical Bengali recipe for chicken and is not complicated to make. The chicken is marinated with spices and then cooked slowly. The result is rich and very tasty. You may recognise it as chicken bhuna.

Mix all the ingredients (apart from the garam masala) together and leave to marinate for about 1 hour.

Heat 2 tablespoons of oil in a large deep pan till hot. Add the chicken, with the marinade. Keep stirring while bringing it to the boil. Cover and cook very slowly for about 45 minutes. Taste and adjust seasoning. Sprinkle with the garam masala, and serve.

Fish Curry

Enough for 3–4 servings

2 tablespoons oil
1 bay leaf
2 small tomatoes cut
   into quarters
Paste made with 1 small onion,
   15g garlic and 15g ginger
1 teaspoon turmeric
½–1 teaspoon red chilli powder
Sugar, a pinch
2cm cinnamon stick
2 cloves
1 cardamom pod
500g fish fillets (tilapia, sea bass,
   cod or haddock)

Just a small piece of cinnamon stick, a cardamom pod and two cloves lend this curry sauce a medley of exciting flavours. It is a fairly thick sauce so you might like to eat the curry with roti or paratha. Otherwise, add a little water, and serve with rice.

Heat the oil in a large pan or wok. When it starts to spit, add the bay leaf, 1 tomato and the onion/garlic/ginger paste. Cook for 3 or 4 minutes while stirring. Now mix in 120ml water, the turmeric, red chilli powder and sugar. Bring to the boil then lower the heat and simmer for 10 minutes, stirring occasionally.

Add the fish and mix in gently. Cover the pan and cook gently for 15 minutes. Taste and adjust the seasoning. You may want to add more chilli, or maybe just some salt. Finally, add the second tomato, the cinnamon, cloves and cardamom, and cook for another 5 minutes.

Fish Curry with Aubergine and Potato

Enough for 6–8 servings

3 tablespoons oil
2 onions, finely chopped
Nigella seed, a pinch
1 large aubergine, cut into thin
   wedges, 5cm long
2 tomatoes, cut into small pieces
3 tablespoons ginger paste
3 tablespoons garlic paste
80g peas, fresh or frozen
2 potatoes, peeled and cut into
   thin wedges, 5cm long

1 teaspoon turmeric
1 teaspoon cumin powder
1 teaspoon coriander powder
¼–1 teaspoon red chilli powder
Sugar, a pinch
½ teaspoon salt
1kg fish fillets (tilapia, sea bass,
   cod or haddock)
Fresh coriander, roughly
   chopped, to garnish

This is a curry for a special occasion. The slivers of white fish are enveloped in a thick delicious sauce that contains juicy aubergine wedges. I have suggested using tilapia as it is a native of West Bengal that is also readily available in the UK. Other types of white fish such as sea bass, cod and haddock work just as well.

Heat the oil in a large pan or wok and fry the chopped onion till it starts to brown. Mix in the nigella seed and fry for a few more minutes. Now add the aubergine wedges and mix well to coat them in oil. Cook for several minutes while stirring. Add the tomato, and ginger and garlic pastes. Mix well and cook for 2–3 minutes. Stir in the peas and potato, and finally the spices. Add 500ml water, the sugar and salt, and bring to the boil. Turn the heat down and simmer for 10–15 minutes until the vegetables are tender. Make sure the aubergine wedges are cooked as they are horrible otherwise! Taste and adjust seasoning.

Cut the fish fillets into 5cm pieces and place on the surface of the sauce. Give them a dusting of salt then cover the pan, and simmer for a further 10 minutes or until the fish is cooked. Garnish with fresh coriander and serve with plain rice.

Fish Curry with Kohlrabi and Potato

Enough for 3–4 servings

2 whole sea bass, cleaned and
    cut into two or three pieces,
    including head and tail
1 teaspoon salt
1 tablespoon turmeric
Oil for frying
2 potatoes, peeled and cut
    into half-moon shapes,
    3mm thick
1 large kohlrabi, peeled and
    cut into half-moon shapes,
    3mm thick
Paste made with 2 onions, 15g
    garlic and 1 dried red chilli
¼–½ teaspoon red chilli
    powder
Fresh coriander, to garnish

Kohlrabi is a typical Bengali – grown vegetable that can be eaten raw or cooked. The taste is similar to that of cabbage and the texture more like turnip. In the UK, you are most likely to be able to buy kohlrabi in specialist greengrocers and the Farmers' Markets that are springing up everywhere. In this recipe, the kohlrabi and potato are cooked with spices to create a tasty substantial sauce, and the pre-fried fish is added at the end. Bengalis are known for using every possible part of everything edible so fish heads and tails are included.

Sprinkle the fish all over with 1 teaspoon salt and ½ tablespoon of the turmeric. Heat a deep pan or wok containing oil to a depth of 3cm. Fry the fish for 5 minutes, then remove it from the oil and set aside.

Heat the same pan and 2 tablespoons of the same oil, and add the potato and kohlrabi, followed by the onion/garlic/chilli paste. Mix well. Now add the remaining ½ tablespoon turmeric and the red chilli powder. Mix again and cook for 10 minutes, stirring frequently. Add enough water to almost cover the vegetables and bring to the boil. Turn down the heat, cover the pan, and simmer for about 20 minutes. Check the vegetables are cooked. The kohlrabi should be firm but not crunchy. Taste and adjust the seasoning if necessary. Finally, add the fish, and heat through. Garnish with fresh coriander and serve with plain rice.

Fish Cutlets in a Spiced Gravy – Macher Jhal

Enough for 3–4 servings

2 whole sea bass, cut into
 2cm wide cutlets
1 teaspoon turmeric, plus
 extra for sprinkling
½ teaspoon salt, plus extra
 for sprinkling
Cumin seed, a pinch
2 large potatoes, cut into
 fingers, 1cm wide
1 teaspoon cumin powder
1 teaspoon ginger paste
4 green chillies, finely sliced
Oil, for frying

West Bengal is well provided with freshwater rivers and lakes, and fish is plentiful here. It is on the Future Hope dinner menu about twice a week. I have vivid memories of squatting on the floor alongside a gaggle of small girls, unusually quiet, as they picked intently among the bones of the fish in front of them, savouring every mouthful. The local fish in Kolkata tends to be exceptionally full of bones though it is exceedingly succulent and tasty. Macher jhal is a typical Bengali dish. The pieces of fish are accompanied by a gravy that is flavoured with cumin and ginger. I have found that sea bass works well in this recipe.

First sprinkle the fish cutlets with salt and turmeric, using just enough to give the cutlets a light covering all over. Leave for about 30 minutes to allow the flavours to infuse.

Heat a large pan or wok containing oil to a depth of about 3cm. When it starts to sizzle, add the fish cutlets and fry for about 5 minutes, turning in the middle. You will probably have to do this in two or three batches. Gently remove the cutlets from the oil taking care that they do not break. Set aside on a plate.

To make the sauce, use just 2 tablespoons of the oil that you used to fry the fish. Heat it

in the pan and add the cumin seed. As soon as the seed starts to brown add the potato. Swish it gently around in the pan so that each individual piece gets coated in oil. Then add the ginger paste, the cumin powder, the green chilli and 1 teaspoon turmeric. Fry for a few minutes and keep stirring to ensure the potato does not stick to the bottom of the pan. Now add enough water to almost cover the potato, and cook gently until the potato is tender but still firm.

Finally, lay the fish gently on top of the potato, cover the pan, and cook on a low heat for 10 minutes. Serve with plain rice or chapati.

Black Chickpeas with Pumpkin and Coconut

Enough for 8 servings

- 100g black chickpeas, soaked and boiled until soft
- 2 tablespoons oil
- 10g ginger paste
- 1 bay leaf
- 1 dried red chilli
- Panchphoran, a big pinch
- 50g desiccated coconut
- 750g pumpkin, cut into 2cm chunks
- 500g potato, peeled and cut into 2cm chunks
- ½ teaspoon turmeric
- ½ teaspoon cumin powder
- ¼ teaspoon red chilli powder
- ¼ teaspoon sugar
- ½ teaspoon salt
- 1 teaspoon ghee

This is one of the few Future Hope recipes with coconut, an ingredient mostly associated with South Indian food. At Future Hope, the cooks use whole coconut that they grate. But desiccated coconut which is easy to buy in the UK works perfectly well. Black chickpeas are slightly smaller than their more common pale yellow cousins but the taste is similar. In fact, they are not really black but a dark red or brown colour. The combination of nutty chickpeas, succulent chunks of pumpkin and flakes of coconut, all coated in spices is stunning.

Soak the chickpeas in a large saucepan of water for 12 hours or overnight. Then drain and wash thoroughly. Put them back in the saucepan with plenty of fresh water. Bring to the boil and simmer till the chickpeas are tender. Drain and set aside.

Heat the oil in a large pan or wok. Add the ginger paste, bay leaf, dried red chilli, panchphoran, chickpeas and coconut. Cook gently for 5 minutes. Add the pumpkin, potato, turmeric, cumin, chilli powder, sugar and salt, and enough water to almost cover. Bring to the boil, cover the pan, turn the heat down and cook gently for 20–30 minutes until the vegetables are cooked. Taste and adjust seasoning. Add the ghee, and serve.

Cauliflower Cooked with Rice, Cashew Nuts and Sultanas – Chal Fulkopi

Serves 8

100ml oil

1 cauliflower, cut into
  small florets

Cumin seed, a pinch

1 bay leaf

25g short grain rice

20g cashew nuts, roughly
  chopped

1 potato, peeled and cut into
  15mm squares

25g ginger paste

¼–1 teaspoon red chilli powder

1 tablespoon cumin powder

½ teaspoon sugar

½ teaspoon salt

250g peas, fresh or frozen

20g sultanas

25g butter

1–2 teaspoons garam masala

The list of ingredients looks scarily long but this is really a recipe worth trying. It is spicy but also sweet due to the sultanas; soft but also crunchy due to the nuts; and moist and comforting. At Future Hope, the short grain rice with the enchanting name Gobindo bhog is used, but pudding rice or risotto rice works perfectly well.

Heat the oil in a large pan or wok and lightly fry the cauliflower florets for a few minutes, stirring all the time. Remove the cauliflower from the oil with a slotted spoon and turn into a sieve. Leave to drain.

Discard all but 2 tablespoons of the oil. Heat it again and add the cumin seed, bay leaf, rice and cashew nuts, and stir well. Cook a few minutes. Stir in the potato, ginger paste, red chilli powder, cumin powder, sugar, salt, and peas. Mix again, and cook a few more minutes. Finally add 250ml water, and the sultanas and cauliflower. Bring to the boil then cover the pan. Lower the heat and simmer until all the vegetables are cooked. Taste and adjust seasoning if necessary. Add the butter and sprinkle with the garam masala before serving.

Chickpeas with Tomato and Spices – Chana Dal

For 6–8 servings

**200g dried chickpeas
2 tablespoons oil
Paste made with 2 onions, 20g
    garlic and 7g ginger
2 large, or 4 small tomatoes,
    cut into 1/8ths
1 teaspoon cumin powder
¼–1 teaspoon red chilli powder
1 teaspoon coriander powder
1 teaspoon turmeric
1 tablespoon garam masala
    (optional)**

This staple dish of Indian cuisine is very nutritious, and quick and easy to make. It is eaten hot or cold, and as part of a meal or a substantial snack. You can shorten the preparation time by using tinned chickpeas, which are readily available and cheap. Make sure to rinse them well before adding to the sauce. Alternatively, use split chickpeas, chana dal, which do not need soaking at all.

First soak the chickpeas for 8 hours or overnight. Strain and wash thoroughly, then boil until tender.

Heat the oil in a large pan or wok. Now add the onion/garlic/ginger paste. Cook for a few minutes, stirring from time to time. Then add the chopped tomato and cumin, chilli and coriander powders and turmeric. Mix well and cook for about 10 minutes. Finally, add the chick peas together with 100ml water, and boil fast for a further 10 minutes. Most of the water will evaporate but you can always add more if you like. Sprinkle with garam masala powder, and serve with a bread such as chapati, poori or paratha.

Rice and Lentils Cooked with Vegetables and Spice – Khichuri

Enough for 4–6 servings

100g short grain rice
100g red lentils
2 tablespoons oil
Cumin seed, a pinch
1 bay leaf
½ dried red chilli
2 potatoes, cut into
   small squares
½ teaspoon cumin
   powder
½ teaspoon turmeric
½ teaspoon red
   chilli powder

½ teaspoon salt
Sugar, a pinch
½ green chilli
100g peas, fresh
   or frozen
½ cauliflower, cut
   into florets
Garam masala, a pinch

Bengali comfort food for a rainy day, khichuri is a wholesome dish full of flavour that is considered a great delicacy. It is purported to have inspired the Anglo-Indian dish Kedgeree. This version of khichuri uses red lentils but you can also try the recipe with split yellow mung beans instead of red lentils – or a mixture of the two – for a slightly different texture and flavour. Khichuri is delicious served with poppadoms and tomato chutney.

Wash the rice and red lentils thoroughly and leave in a sieve to drain.

Heat the oil in a large pan or wok. First add the cumin seed, then the bay leaf and the dried red chilli. Cook a minute or two then add the potato. Stir well. Still stirring, add the rice and the dal then the cumin powder, turmeric, red chilli powder, salt and sugar.

Mix everything and fry a few minutes. Add 500ml water and bring to the boil. Finally add the green chilli, peas and cauliflower. Cover the pan and turn the heat down. Simmer on a low heat until everything is cooked. Taste and adjust seasoning. Sprinkle with the garam masala and serve.

Yellow Peas with Meat and Spices – Ghugni

Enough for 8 servings

250g dried yellow peas
125g lamb or mutton
2 tablespoons oil
1 onion, chopped finely
1 dried red chilli
1 bay leaf
Paste made with 1 onion,
  10g garlic, 10g ginger and
  5g green chilli

½ teaspoon cumin powder
2½ teaspoons coriander powder
1 green chilli, cut into
  fine rounds
1 tomato, roughly chopped

If you walk around Kolkata at any time of day or night, the choice of freshly-cooked street food is overwhelming. Ghugni is invariably on the menu. A typically Bengali snack, ghugni is essentially a mix of yellow peas and spices, with or without flakes of meat. The older boys at Future Hope's Bompass Home make many kilos of ghugni for the end-of-year Mela. It is considered a real treat. Dried yellow peas are not always easy to find in the UK but you can always use chickpeas or other dried peas instead.

Soak the yellow peas in a large saucepan of water for 12 hours or overnight. Drain and wash thoroughly. Put them back in the saucepan with plenty of fresh water. Bring to the boil and simmer until the yellow peas are tender. Drain and set aside.

Boil or braise the lamb or mutton with a little water until cooked. Let it cool then chop very finely with a sharp knife. Mix the meat with the peas.

Heat the oil in a large pan or wok and fry the chopped onion until it starts to brown. Add all the other ingredients, apart from the peas and meat. Mix well, and cook for 10 minutes. Finally add the peas and meat with 200ml water. Bring to the boil then reduce heat and cook gently for 30 minutes. Taste and adjust seasoning.

Aubergine Mash with Garlic and Ginger – Begun Bharta

Enough for 2–4 servings

2 medium aubergines
2 tablespoons olive oil
1 onion, finely chopped
2 cloves garlic, finely chopped
20g ginger, finely chopped
2 medium tomatoes,
   cut into 1cm pieces
½ teaspoon salt
2 tablespoons fresh
   coriander, roughly
   chopped

This is a soft, mushy and extremely tasty way of cooking aubergine that you can include as part of a meal, or eat as a snack at any time of the day, hot or cold, with a fresh steaming roti. One of the few recipes that has no chilli, this bharta gets its 'kick' from garlic and ginger. I am most grateful to my friend Ranjana for this recipe. A teacher at Future Hope, now retired, she took care of children who were newly arrived at the school, helping them to find their feet and 'fast-track' to the class appropriate to their age.

First prepare the aubergines. They need to be cooked until the skin is black and blistering, and the inside is soft and tender. The way to do this is to halve the aubergines along their length, place the halves flesh side down on a foil lined grill pan and cook them under a very hot grill. Alternatively, you can cook them over a flame. You will have to put a skewer through the centre of each aubergine and then hold it over the flame turning slowly.

Once the aubergines have cooled a bit, scoop the flesh out of the 'burnt' skin and roughly chop it.

Now gently cook the finely chopped onion in the olive oil for about 10 minutes until it becomes transparent. Mix in the garlic and ginger and cook for a further 3 or 4 minutes. Finally, add the tomatoes and salt. Continue cooking gently until the tomatoes soften then add the chopped aubergine flesh and cook for a further 5 minutes. Taste and adjust seasoning.

Sprinkle with the coriander, and serve.

Aubergine, Fried
– Begun Bhaja

Enough for 2–4 servings

2 aubergines
500ml oil
Turmeric, a sprinkling
Salt, a sprinkling
Sugar, a sprinkling

Cut the aubergines into longitudinal segments. You will probably obtain 6 or 8 segments from each one. Lightly sprinkle the cut sides of the aubergine with turmeric, salt and sugar, and rub it in gently. Set aside for 5–10 minutes. Meanwhile, heat the oil in a large deep pan until it starts to sizzle. Fry the aubergine segments in the hot oil, turning over to ensure they are cooked all the way through. They will turn a deep golden brown. Drain and lay on a bed of absorbent kitchen paper. Serve.

Aubergine Slices, Battered and Fried – Beguni

Enough for 4–6 servings

2 aubergines, cut into slices
  3–4mm thick
250g gram flour
Bicarbonate of soda, a pinch
Red chilli powder, a pinch
½ teaspoon sugar
1 teaspoon salt
500ml oil

Juicy, succulent aubergine slices in a crispy light batter, so simple and so delicious, these beguni are a real treat. Try the variation, using the same batter but vegetables such as cauliflower, green pepper, potato and pumpkin, instead of aubergine.

Sieve the bicarbonate of soda, sugar, salt, chilli powder and gram flour together. Add enough water (about 250ml) to form a smooth batter that has a coating consistency. Now heat the oil in a large deep pan until it starts to sizzle. Dip the aubergine slices into the batter, making sure they are thoroughly coated with it, and fry them in small batches in the hot oil until they are completely cooked and turn a deep golden brown. Remove the beguni from the oil and transfer to a bed of absorbent kitchen paper. Serve with tomato chutney.

PAKORA

Try the same recipe with small pieces of cauliflower, potato, green pepper or pumpkin instead of aubergine, to make the very popular Indian snack pakora. The batter is the same and so is the method of frying, although some vegetables will take longer to cook than others.

Enough for 4–6 servings

FOR THE KOPTA
2 green bananas (unripe ones)
1 teaspoon turmeric
1 teaspoon oil
100g flour
½ teaspoon salt
1 teaspoon cumin seed
1 teaspoon garam masala
   powder
1 teaspoon black peppercorns
50ml oil for frying

FOR THE SAUCE
1 onion, finely chopped
Paste made with 15g garlic and
   25g ginger
1 teaspoon cumin powder
½ teaspoon red chilli powder
1 teaspoon turmeric

Banana Balls in a Curry Sauce – Kopta Curry

Bengali cuisine makes the most of the abundant fresh produce that grows in the region, whether it is ripe, or not. Unripe fruit such as papaya and banana often forms the basis for savoury recipes. Kopta curry is one example. The green unripe bananas are made into small fried balls (kopta) that taste delicious but not particularly of banana. They are served in a tasty curry sauce.

Cook the whole unpeeled bananas in boiling water and a teaspoon each of turmeric and oil for about 20 minutes until the bananas become soft. Peel and mash them.

Heat the cumin seed, garam masala and black peppercorns in a dry pan until they start to smell. Take the pan off the heat, and grind the spices to a powder. Mix a pinch of this powder with the mashed banana and keep the rest for later.

Mix the flour with the mashed banana and add the salt. Taste and add more salt or ground spices if you want. Form the mixture into small balls and fry in hot oil until they turn deep brown. Remove from the oil.

To make the sauce, fry the chopped onion in the remaining oil until it starts to brown. Add the garlic and ginger paste, and continue to fry for another three or four minutes. Now add the cumin powder, chilli powder and turmeric. Mix well. Add a little salt and 500ml water. Bring to the boil, reduce heat, and simmer until the sauce smells nice. Put the fried banana balls in the sauce and serve with a sprinkling of the ground spices.

Cabbage Cooked with Potato and Bengali Spices – Cabbage Chechki

I am particularly fond of cabbage and this typical Bengali way of preparing cabbage is especially effective. While spices are added in the cooking, the basic cabbage taste and texture is enhanced rather than overwhelmed by them. Panchphoran, the spice that flavours cabbage chechki is a mixture of 5 spices (cumin seed, fenugreek seed, black mustard seed, fennel seed and onion seed). It is readily available in the UK. Kolkata cabbages are green and quite firm but you can make this dish with whichever variety you have available. I usually use a firm white one.

Enough for 4–6 servings

50ml oil
½–1 dried red chilli
Panchphoran, a pinch
500g white or green cabbage,
    roughly chopped
1 very large potato or two
    medium ones, cut into 4mm
    thick slices

1 green chilli
1 bay leaf
1 teaspoon sugar
½ teaspoon salt

Heat the oil in a deep pan then add the red chilli and panchphoran and cook for about 2 minutes. Now mix the cabbage with the oil and cook for a few minutes until it wilts a bit. Add all the other ingredients and sufficient water to almost cover the vegetables. Bring to the boil. Cover the pan and reduce the heat. Let it simmer until the potato is cooked, which will take about 15 minutes. If there seems to be a lot of liquid, increase the heat at the end and boil fast for a minute or two to reduce it. Taste and adjust seasoning.

Enough for 6–8 servings

50ml oil
1 onion, finely chopped
½ tablespoon turmeric
1 bay leaf

Cabbage Curry 1

1 teaspoon salt
2 small salad potatoes cut
   into 2cm chunks
½ teaspoon sugar
¼–½ teaspoon red chilli powder
500g cabbage, finely sliced
250g peas, fresh or frozen

This is a typical Future Hope lunchtime dish that is much loved. Not just tasty but also quick and easy to make. Use whichever type of cabbage you have available. For a special treat, add prawns (see below).

First heat the oil in a deep pan. Add the onion, turmeric, bay leaf and salt, and cook gently until the onion starts to brown. Now, mix in the potato and coat with the oil. Then add all the other ingredients together with 250ml of water. Bring to the boil, turn the heat down, cover and simmer for about 20 minutes, until the potato is cooked.

CABBAGE AND PRAWN CURRY

Lightly fry 250g prawns then add to the curry at the same time as the potato. Otherwise the recipe is the same.

Cabbage Curry 2

Enough for 6–8 servings

50ml oil
250g potato, peeled and
  cut into 1cm squares
500g cabbage, shredded
1 teaspoon ginger paste
½ teaspoon salt
½ teaspoon turmeric
1 bay leaf
1 tomato, diced
150g peas
½ teaspoon sugar
¼–½ teaspoon red chilli powder
Garam masala, a large pinch

Quite similar to Cabbage Curry 1, this recipe contains tomato and ginger but no onion, and it cooks in its own juices without the addition of water. Try them both and see which one you prefer.

Heat the oil in a very large deep pan. Stir in the potato and cabbage, ensuring they are lightly coated in oil. Cook for a few minutes. Add the ginger paste, salt and turmeric, and mix well. Then add the bay leaf, tomato, peas and sugar. Finally stir in the chilli powder. Cover the pan and cook gently for about 30 minutes, or until all the vegetables are cooked. Taste and adjust seasoning. Before serving sprinkle with a large pinch of garam masala powder.

Cauliflower Curry

Enough for 4–6 servings

This is a tasty cauliflower dish that is richly flavoured with cumin.

1 cauliflower, split into
  2cm florets
100ml oil
Cumin seed, a pinch
1 bay leaf
1 large potato, peeled or
  unpeeled, cut into 2cm chunks
½ tablespoon ginger paste
½ tablespoon cumin powder
¼–1 teaspoon red chilli powder
½ teaspoon salt
½ teaspoon sugar
½ teaspoon garam masala

Heat the oil in a big pan or wok and fry the cauliflower florets for a few minutes, stirring all the time. Remove the cauliflower from the oil with a slotted spoon, and turn into a sieve. Set aside, and leave to drain.

Heat just two tablespoons of the remaining oil in a big pan and add the cumin seed, bay leaf and potato. Mix well. Then add the ginger paste and cumin powder, chilli powder, salt and sugar. Mix well and cook for 5 minutes. Add enough water to just cover the potato. Bring to the boil then lower heat, cover pan and simmer for 10 minutes. Uncover the pan, add the cauliflower and simmer until all the vegetables are cooked. Finally add the garam masala, and serve.

Enough for 6–8 servings

100ml oil
1 large cauliflower,
  cut into small florets
1 bay leaf
½ teaspoon cumin seed
2 green chillies, slit lengthwise
1 large potato, peeled and
  cut into 1cm cubes
1 large tomato,
  cut into 1cm pieces

40g peas, fresh or frozen
1 teaspoon cumin powder
¼–1 teaspoon red chilli powder
½ teaspoon turmeric
½ teaspoon sugar
½ teaspoon salt
Small bunch fresh coriander,
  roughly chopped

Cauliflower Florets in a Spiced Gravy

This is a rare recipe that contains no onion, garlic or ginger. But there are still plenty of spices to give an exceptionally tasty gravy.

Heat the oil in a large pan or wok and fry the cauliflower florets for a few minutes, stirring all the time. Remove the cauliflower with a slotted spoon and turn into a sieve. Set aside and leave to drain.

Using just 2 tablespoons of the remaining oil, fry the bay leaf and cumin seed for about a minute. Add the green chilli, potato, tomato and peas. Mix well and cook for another minute. Add the cumin powder, chilli powder, turmeric, sugar and salt. Mix well, turn heat down and cook gently for 10 minutes. Finally add the cauliflower and enough water to almost cover the vegetables. Bring to the boil then turn the heat down, cover the pan and simmer for another 10 minutes, or until all the vegetables are cooked. Taste and adjust seasoning. Garnish with coriander and serve.

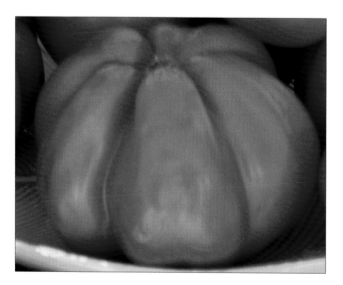

Cauliflower Florets with Potato, Peas and Bengali Spices – Aloo Fulkopir Chechki

Enough for 4–6 servings

100ml oil
1 small cauliflower, cut into small
  florets
¼ teaspoon panchphoran
1 large tomato or 2 small,
  chopped into 1/8ths
½ teaspoon ginger paste
250g potato, peeled and cut into
  2cm chunks
100g peas, fresh or frozen
½ teaspoon salt
1 teaspoon cumin powder
¼ teaspoon turmeric
¼–½ teaspoon red chilli powder
1 green chilli, cut into
  fine rounds
½ teaspoon sugar
Small bunch fresh coriander,
  washed and roughly chopped

Another typical Bengali recipe using panchphoran, the vegetables in this dish swim in a delicious gravy.

Heat the oil in a large pan or wok and fry the cauliflower florets for a few minutes, stirring all the time. Remove the cauliflower from the oil with a slotted spoon and turn into a sieve. Set aside and leave to drain.

Heat just 3 tablespoons of the remaining oil in the pan. Add the panchphoran, tomato and ginger paste. Stir and cook for a few minutes. Mix in the cauliflower, potato and peas, and cook for a few minutes. Add the salt, cumin powder, turmeric, red chilli powder, green chilli and sugar, and cook for a few minutes. Pour in 100ml water and bring to the boil. Cover the pan and reduce the heat. Simmer for about 10 minutes, stirring from time to time. When the potato and cauliflower are just tender, stir in the coriander and serve.

Mixed Vegetable Curry

Enough for 6–8 servings

3 tablespoons oil
Nigella seed, a pinch
1–3 dried red chillies
500g potato, cut into 2cm
  chunks, not necessarily peeled
½ teaspoon salt
1 teaspoon cumin powder
½ tablespoon turmeric
Sugar, a pinch
500g pumpkin, cut into 2cm
  chunks
500g sim – or mangetout

Mixed vegetable dishes usually contain at least three different kinds of vegetable, one of which is always potato. The Bengalis love their potato. It is in almost all of the savoury recipes in this book. But they also love pumpkin, carrot, cauliflower and….sim. Sim are giant-sized mangetout. If you have sim to use in this recipe, you will need to cut them into two or three pieces. Otherwise use whole mangetout.

Heat the oil in a large pan or wok and briefly fry the nigella seed and dried red chillies, then the potato. Stir well to coat with oil, and cook a few minutes. Add the salt, cumin, turmeric and sugar, and stir. Then add the pumpkin and sim/mangetout. Stir again. Finally, add 120ml water, bring to the boil then reduce heat, cover and cook very slowly until all the vegetables are tender. It will take about 20 minutes. Taste and adjust the seasoning before serving.

You can also make this curry with a mix of vegetables that includes aubergine, carrot and cauliflower. It is best to pre-cook the aubergine and the cauliflower in a small amount of oil for about 5 minutes and to add them to the mix about 10 minutes before the end of the cooking time. With carrot, small pieces are best as it takes a long time to cook.

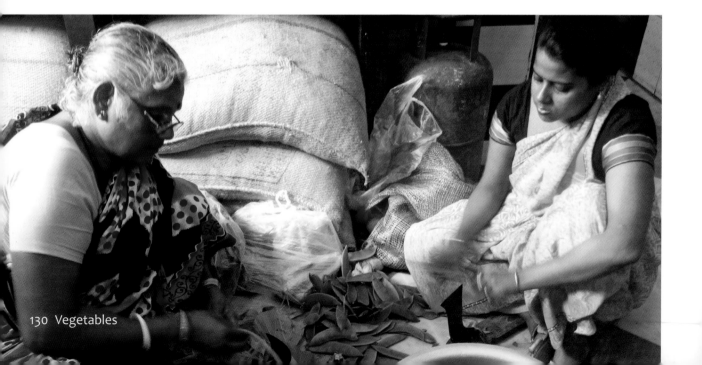

Enough for 8–10 servings

50ml oil
1 small onion, finely chopped
Nigella seed, a pinch
½–1 dried red chilli
½ teaspoon turmeric
1kg vegetables, cut into
matchsticks 3cm long,
4mm wide

Make this dish with the vegetables of your choice. At Future Hope, the mix usually includes potato and two others, which could be beetroot and kohlrabi, carrot and green beans, or cauliflower and green beans. The colours are all-important.

Heat the oil in a large pan or wok and fry the onion until it starts to brown. Mix in the nigella seed, red chilli and turmeric, and cook for a few more minutes. Now add all the vegetables and a sprinkling of salt. Stir well so that all the vegetables are lightly coated in oil. Cover the pan and cook on a low heat, stirring regularly, until all the vegetables are cooked. This could take 45 minutes or even 1 hour. Add a little water if the vegetables start to stick to the bottom of the pan. Taste and adjust seasoning.

Enough for 6 servings

3 tablespoons oil
250g onions, cut into 1cm pieces
50g garlic, made into paste
50g fresh ginger, made
   into paste
125g carrot, diced very small
1 large head broccoli, separated
   into very small florets
½ teaspoon sugar
40ml distilled malt vinegar
40ml soy sauce
2 green chillies, slit lengthwise
125g green pepper,
   cut into 1cm pieces
50g salad onion leaves,
   cut into 2cm lengths
450g mushrooms,
   cut into 1/8ths
½ teaspoon salt
Black pepper

Chilli Mushroom

Mushrooms are more associated with Chinese cuisine than with Indian. However, enterprising houseparent Basudev started cultivating oyster mushrooms at Ballygunge Boys' Home and they now feature on Future Hope menus. Basudev first experimented on a small scale. He then set up more than 25 mushroom beds in an empty store room at the Home, and harvested an incredible 75kg of mushrooms over a 4–5 month period. Here is the recipe that Basudev and the boys made for the 2014 Future Hope Mela festivities. Oyster mushrooms are very expensive in the UK so I have cooked this recipe with common closed-cup mushrooms and it is really delicious.

First heat the oil and fry the onion until it just starts to brown. Mix in the garlic and ginger pastes and continue cooking until they go brown, stirring frequently. Add the carrot and broccoli, and cook for another 10 minutes. Now add the sugar, vinegar, soy sauce, green chilli, green pepper, onion leaves and mushrooms. Mix well, cover the pan and cook gently until all the vegetables are tender, stirring from time to time. Adjust seasoning, if necessary. Before serving, sprinkle with freshly ground black pepper.

Bengali Boiled Potato with Tomato, Peas, and Spices – Sanjib's Aloo Dum

Enough for 8 servings

2kg small round potatoes
4 tablespoons oil
5 teaspoons ginger/
   garlic paste
200g onion, made into a paste
¼–1½ teaspoons red chilli
   powder
1 teaspoon turmeric
2 tomatoes, chopped
250g peas, fresh or frozen
Coriander to decorate

This is a typical Bengali recipe for potatoes. You can even buy 'aloo dum' potatoes at the market. I am grateful to senior Future Hope student Sanjib who gave me the recipe. Aloo dum is Sanjib's signature dish at Ballygunge Boys' home where the boys take turns at cooking Sunday meals. Aloo dum potatoes are small, round and firm. A waxy new potato such as Charlotte would work well in this recipe.

Boil the potatoes in salted water until firm. Drain and, once cool, remove the skins.

Heat the oil in a large saucepan. When it is hot, add the ginger/garlic paste, and immediately turn the heat down. Add the onion paste and mix. Cook gently for several minutes. Add the red chilli powder, turmeric and chopped tomatoes, and mix again. Cook gently, stirring from time to time, until the mixture turns a brownish red. Now add the peas, then the potatoes. Heat well. Garnish with coriander, and serve.

For an aloo dum with gravy, simply add water at the same time as adding the peas and potato. This is a good idea if you are serving the aloo dum with rice.

Bengali Cubed Potato – Aloo Chorchori

A very simple but effective dish with subtly-flavoured cubes of potato that is often served for lunch at Future Hope.

Enough for 4–6 servings

2 tablespoons oil
Nigella seed, a pinch
500g potatoes, peeled and cut
    into 1cm cubes
250g peas, fresh or frozen
½ teaspoon sugar
½ teaspoon salt
Fresh coriander, washed and
    roughly chopped, to garnish

Heat the oil in a large pan or wok and add the nigella seed. Allow it to fry for a minute or two. Mix in the potato, peas, sugar and salt. Cook gently for a few minutes stirring continuously to prevent the potato sticking to the bottom of the pan. Now add enough water to almost cover the potato. Bring to the boil, then reduce heat and simmer while the potato cooks. Taste and adjust seasoning. Garnish with coriander leaf and serve.

Bengali Jewish-Style Potatoes – Aloo Makallah

Trading opportunities brought Jews from Baghdad to Kolkata in the early 19th Century. This is one of the community's standard recipes and I have my friend Flower to thank for it. She specifies that the potatoes should be a little larger than a very large egg. They should also be the type of 'old' potato most suitable for making French fries, such as King Edward or Maris Piper. Cooked this way, the potatoes have a crust that is very hard and crispy, and an inside that is deliciously soft and succulent.

20 potatoes
1 tablespoon salt
1 tablespoon turmeric
1 litre oil

Firstly peel the potatoes. Now fill a large pan with water adding the salt and turmeric. Bring the water to the boil and put the potatoes in. As soon as the water comes back to the boil, take it off the heat and drain the potatoes. Leave them to cool.

Using the same pan, heat the oil and, as soon as it starts to spit, put the potatoes in. There should be enough oil to cover the potatoes. Gently boil the potatoes in the oil until they form a thin yellow crust. Turn off the heat and leave to cool, with the potatoes staying in the oil. As soon as they are cool enough to handle, prick the potatoes three or four times with a skewer and replace in the cold oil. Leave them there for a few hours or overnight.

About 1 hour before you want to serve the potatoes, put the pan back on the stove and heat gently. When the oil comes to the boil, continue cooking for a further 20 minutes. The potatoes will be brown and crispy hard.

Bengali Mashed Potato with Coriander, Onion and Tomato – Aloo Chokha

Enough for 6–8 servings

1kg potato, peeled and
   boiled
2 tomatoes, chopped
4 small green chillies,
   finely sliced into rings

2 onions, finely sliced
25ml oil
A handful of coriander,
   finely chopped
Salt to taste

This is mashed potato with a difference. A cross between a European-style mashed potato and potato salad, aloo chokha is full of interesting textures and flavours. In Bengali homes, mustard oil is the norm and this gives aloo chokha a distinctive flavour. In the UK, mustard oil is rarely used. But, even without mustard oil, this potato dish is delicious.

Mash the potatoes roughly. Then mix in all the other ingredients, mashing a little bit more. It is now ready to eat.

Carrot Halwa with Cashews, Almonds and Cardamom – Gajar Halwa

Enough for 12–16 portions

3 cardamom pods
100g ghee
1kg carrots, peeled and
    finely grated
100g sugar
200g condensed milk (tinned)
150g cashew nuts or almonds, or
    a mixture, finely chopped
50g desiccated coconut

Packed with the goodness of carrots, this sweet and soft, creamy and crunchy dessert is widely available in restaurants and confectionery stores in Kolkata. You can eat it hot. Or leave it to chill and cut into squares and serve as petit fours! This version of the recipe uses tinned condensed milk that is easily found in the UK. It replaces khowa, one of India's many amazing milk products.

Remove the seeds from the cardamom pods and grind them to a powder using a pestle and mortar.

Gently heat half the ghee (50g) in a large pan. When it has melted, add the grated carrot and cook for a couple of minutes, stirring gently. Add the sugar a spoonful at a time, stirring after each addition. Continue cooking the mixture gently, and stirring, until the liquid that has formed in the bottom of the pan has almost all evaporated. Mix in the rest of the ghee, the condensed milk and the ground cardamom. Finally add the nuts. Serve hot or cold. For serving cold, pack the mixture into a large square dish then chill and cut into squares.

GHEE

It is not a problem to find ghee in UK supermarkets but it is also easy to make at home, and it will taste much nicer. Simply melt 250g unsalted butter over a gentle heat. Do not stir at any stage. Keep the butter simmering gently for about 20 minutes. During the process, a white foam forms on the surface of the butter and the milk solids collect at the bottom of the pan. Once the molten butter is completely transparent, remove the pan from the heat and leave to cool for about 20 minutes. Now gently skim the frothy layer off the surface of the ghee and discard. Then, let the contents of the pan settle before pouring most of it through a sieve. But discard the last few drops containing the fine dregs of the milk solids. A 250g block of butter produces about 180g ghee.

Chocolate Biscuit Crumb Balls

Makes about 24 balls

225g digestive biscuits
  (or other plain biscuit)
50g raisins
200g plain chocolate
45ml honey or syrup
50g butter
Biscuit crumbs, desiccated
  coconut, cocoa or chopped
  nuts, for coating

I brought this no-bake recipe for chocolate balls to Kolkata to make with the children at Future Hope. The balls are messy and fun for children to roll. And extremely chocolatey. Good for every occasion. I have many happy memories of making them with the small girls at Rowland Road and with the Ballygunge boys. The adults-only variation with rum is really good too.

First crush the biscuits till you have a bowl of crumbs. You can do this by breaking the biscuits into a bowl and simply crushing with your fingers. Or you can seal the biscuits in a large plastic bag and bash them with a rolling pin. Mix in the raisins. Using a separate bowl, melt the chocolate, honey or syrup and butter over a saucepan of boiling water. Now stir the biscuit crumbs into the chocolate mixture. Leave for 30 minutes to solidify slightly in the fridge. Pinch off small chunks of the mixture and form into balls the size of a walnut. Roll in biscuit crumbs, desiccated coconut, chopped nuts or cocoa. Chill again.

FOR RUM BALLS

Soak the raisins in a small bowl with enough rum to just cover them, for about 24 hours. Then add the raisins to the recipe as above (together with any rum that has not been absorbed). The rest of the recipe is the same.

Fruit Chaat with Yoghurt and Cardamom

Fruit chaat is a fruit salad with a sweet yoghurt dressing and a mild spicy flavouring. You can make it with almost any fruit. In Kolkata, apples, mangoes and pomegranates are inexpensive and readily available, and are highly suitable for this chaat. I've used blueberries, grapes and kiwi fruit too. As for the yoghurt (or curd, as Indians call it) any unflavoured one is suitable.

Enough for 8–10 servings

200g sugar
750g yoghurt
2 mangoes
1 pomegranate
50g cherries
2 apples
Grapes, blueberries, kiwi fruit...

Saffron, a pinch (optional)
8 cardamom pods, seeds removed
and finely ground

Stir the sugar into the yoghurt. Cover the bowl and put in the refrigerator to chill. Now wash and prepare all the fruit: stone the cherries, core the apples, remove the pith from the pomegranate seeds, cut grapes in half and take out the pips. The apples can be left with the peel on if you like. Cut apple and mango and kiwi into small 1cm pieces. Gently stir the fruit into the yoghurt with the saffron. Sprinkle with the ground cardamom seeds, and serve.

You can use a pestle and mortar to grind the cardamom seeds, or a spice grinder. Or, you can buy cardamom 'powder', but freshly-ground spice always has the best flavour.

Fruit chaat keeps well in the refrigerator for a day or two.

YOGHURT (CURD)

It is simple and fun to make your own yoghurt. First you need to heat a litre of milk very gently until it is 'hand' hot, so if you dip a finger in it, it will feel hot but not burning. Now stir in a tablespoon of ready-made 'live' yoghurt, and put in a warm place for 12–24 hours to set. On a hot day, you can just leave the mixture on a sunny window sill. Once the yoghurt has set, you can thicken it if you like by draining it in a sieve lined with a piece of muslin.

Rice Pudding with Cardamom – Payes

Enough for 8 servings

1 litre milk, full fat or half fat
100g pudding rice
1 tablespoon sugar
1 or 2 cardamom pods, bruised
1 or 2 bay leaves
50g sultanas (optional)
50g cashew nuts (optional)

This Indian version of a rice pudding graces the table on very special occasions such as birthdays, religious festivals or the arrival of an honoured guest, also to celebrate a new home or new clothes. With subtle aromatic flavouring from cardamom and bay leaves, and a long slow cooking time, payes is an exceptionally creamy and tasty dessert. My thanks to houseparent Bandana for this recipe. She uses a type of rice that goes by the charismatic name of gobindo bhog. It's not readily available in the UK but regular short grain pudding rice works perfectly well.

Gently warm the milk in a large saucepan, and very gradually bring to the boil. This might take 40 minutes. In the meantime, wash the rice thoroughly and drain.

Once the milk has started to boil, add the rice, and stir well to prevent it sticking to the bottom of the pan. Now, simmer very gently, stirring regularly, until the rice starts to appear at the surface of the milk. This takes about an hour. Add the sugar, cardamom and bay leaves. Stir well and cook gently for a further 10 minutes. Taste and add more sugar if you want.

Cook a further 15 minutes. Finally add the sultanas and/or cashew nuts if you are using them. The payes will still be quite liquid but it will thicken up as it cools. Eat hot or cold.

Roasted Chickpea Fudge – Sattu Laddu

When the children at Future Hope offered me my first sattu laddu, I thought it was out-of-this-world. The combination of the roasted flour, the cardamom and the ghee gives a wondrous flavour.

Enough for about 10 laddu

120g gram flour
100g ghee, at room temperature
80g icing sugar
½ teaspoon cardamom powder

First you need to roast the gram flour by heating it in a clean dry frying pan. Use a gentle heat, and keep stirring the flour as it cooks. It will gradually change colour from its original buttercup yellow to a deep sandy brown. This is chana sattu. It will have lost a bit of weight during the cooking process. You need 100g for the recipe so check the weight of the roasted flour and discard any excess before making the laddu.

To make the laddu, combine the chana sattu with the icing sugar and cardamom powder. Now mix with the ghee to create a stiff paste. Form the paste into small balls or patties and put them in the fridge to set.

Coconut Balls with Cardamom – Coconut Laddu

The easiest recipe ever, and huge sticky fun for children to make.

Makes 24 balls

200g desiccated coconut
200g condensed milk (tinned)
½ teaspoon cardamom powder

Combine the cardamom and coconut. Add the condensed milk and mix thoroughly. Using wet hands, form into balls or patties. Chill.

Spiced Milk Tea – Chai

Chai is available on every street corner in India, often served in rough clay goblets that you just chuck in the gutter when empty. At Future Hope, Dulu or Ganga can be seen walking round the school with a huge kettle of chai for the staff in morning and afternoon breaks. Sometimes chai is very weak, sometimes very strong, but usually extremely sweet. Thanks to houseparent Champa for sharing her recipe.

Enough for 4 cups

500ml water
500ml milk
Sugar, to taste
3g fresh ginger, bruised
2 bay leaves
4 tablespoons tea leaves
2 cardamom pods, seeds removed
   and ground

Heat the water, milk, sugar, ginger and bay leaves in a saucepan over a gentle heat, stirring until the sugar has dissolved. Bring to the boil then reduce the heat and simmer for 10 minutes. Add the tea leaves and simmer for 10 minutes. Stir in the ground cardamom seeds. Serve.

Spiced Ginger Chai

Most chai is milky but here is a delicious recipe for chai that has no milk but lots of ginger and cardamom. Thanks to houseparent Bandana for sharing her recipe.

Pour the boiling water onto the tea leaves. Mash with a spoon. Add all the other ingredients, and mash again. Serve.

Enough for 1 cup

250ml boiling water
1 tablespoon tea leaves
14g fresh ginger, bruised
1 cardamom pod, bruised
Sugar, to taste

Index